# COMMON
# SENSE
# &
# TIMING

# COMMON

## & SENSE

## TIMING

*Your Guide to Business and
Social Success*

# Michael J. Cutino

*St. Martin's Press     New York*

Library of Congress Cataloging-in-Publication Data

Cutino, Michael J.
     Common sense and timing : Letting your sixth sense guide you to business success / Michael J. Cutino.—1st ed.
          p.          cm.
     ISBN 0-312-93164-6
     1. Success in business.          I. Title.
HF5386.C94          1990
650.1—dc20                                    90-9063
                                                   CIP

Book design by Judith Stagnitto

Printed in the United States of America
First edition: November 1990
0 9 8 7 6 5 4 3 2 1

*Special thanks to the people at Walt Disney World, Hershey Chocolate Public Relations Department, Cathy Silverstein (my ghostwriter), and my family—Becky, Mikey, Mark, and Brian*

# CONTENTS

*"Nothing astonishes men so much as common sense and plain dealing."*
— Ralph Waldo Emerson, 1841

*"Every step in a positive direction or step forward is a reward in itself."*
— Michael J. Cutino, 1988

*"Failure should never be taken in a negative way. It just gives you the experience for the next time."*
— Michael J. Cutino, 1990

# COMMON
## SENSE
# &
## TIMING

We're all looking for a fast, easy way to live happily ever after—peace of mind and the American dream! We all want success and we want it *now*. There must be something we don't know—a shortcut, a secret, a hint—but it has to be easy, cheap, and not too time-consuming because, Lord knows, everything else in our lives is either difficult or expensive or takes forever.

The way exists: common sense, something we all possess. And if we all have it, why don't we have everything else we want? What's the catch?

The catch is that we don't often use the common sense we're born with. We don't look at all the possibilities. Sometimes we aren't even focusing on the real problem. Often a problem starts out as a small seed and, before you know it, you have a big unwieldy weed on your hands (the proverbial mountain out of a molehill). You can get so involved in identifying the difficulty that you forget about trying to solve it. And when you finally get it all into perspective, you realize it wasn't such a big deal after all. Sometimes your anxiety over what to do is more upsetting than the actual dilemma. This book is intended to help you think smarter, sharper and more logically.

Solving problems is just like shooting pool. Usually there are several angles from which you can shoot the cue ball to hit another ball into the pocket. Think of the cue ball as the action you take to solve a problem; the other balls represent the problem; the pockets are, of course, the answers. Sometimes you aim for the red ball, but you miss and knock another ball into the pocket. The format of the game changes. So it is with life: we cannot always plan consequences, but we can try to cover all the angles. All it takes is careful aim and a little common sense and timing!

*Common Sense and Timing* deals with your mind, your body and how YOU can make the right decision at the right time. The ideas here can help you achieve the independence, confidence and stability for a success-filled future. There are no guarantees in life, and I certainly can't guarantee what results you'll obtain— only that you will indeed get results!

Look at the people around you, the ones in the spotlight, the ones getting things done. If you ask them, you'll find that their success is achieved through common sense and by being at the right place at the right time—that is, timing.

But that's them, you say, not me. Well, it can be

you! No common sense? Nonsense! We're all born with common sense—it's instinctive! What about being in the right place at the right time? Is it just luck? Or is it common sense?

## YOUR SIXTH SENSE

Common sense. Common means everyday. Not special. Ordinary. Ordinary sense. Not extraordinary sense. Nothing exceptional, nothing unusual. It's so obvious we often overlook it.

Sense means understanding or knowledge. We have five basic senses—sight, smell, hearing, taste and touch. These senses contribute to our overall sensitivity.

Then there is our "sixth sense." What is that? You've heard people say, "My sixth sense told me you were going to call," or "I sensed this was going to happen." How did they know this? Do they have a mysterious psychic power? Do angels whisper in their ears? Maybe, but I doubt it. These people are just using all of their senses. That pooling of information, that "sixth sense," is plain old Common Sense. Ordinary knowledge. Everyday understanding.

Belief in your SELF and your SENSE of self-confidence plays a very important role in common SENSE decisions. You can develop an awareness of your emotional personality (a sixth *sense*) and use *all* of your feelings—your loving, giving playful ones; your jealous, angry, vengeful ones; the uncertain, wishful, wistful ones; and the bold, brave, courageous ones—to your benefit.

I will teach you how to direct your body SENSES and to channel them into positive and effective ways of communicating with people. Throughout this book, I will show you how you can use your common sense and timing to make life's everyday problems easier to deal with, easier to solve, easier to dissolve. Applying all those senses into a positive personality flow will give you the confidence to make good decisions at the right time.

## THE *IF ONLYS* AND THE *I'M GLADS*

How often have you heard people say, "If only . . . ?" "If only I were rich . . ." "If only I had listened . . ." "If only I had time . . ." "If only . . ." "If only . . ." "If only . . ."

There are doers and there are talkers. The majority of talkers will "if only" themselves till their dying day! Doers and talkers. Which are you? How many "if onlys" have you collected so far?

And what about the "I'm glad . . ."s? "I'm glad I did . . ." "I'm glad I went . . ." "I'm glad I saw . . ." "I'm glad . . ." "I'm glad . . ." "I'm glad . . ." How many?

Talkers and Doers. Would you rather say, "If only . . ." or "I'm glad I . . ."? I'll tell you, "I'M GLAD I . . . !" I'm glad I wrote this book! I'm glad you picked it up! I'm glad I can help you! I'm glad you want to learn and grow and do the most that you can do! The world needs more like us!

I didn't start out rich and famous. I grew up in Queens in the fifties. My mom was a housewife. My dad was a sanitation engineer (back then we called them garbagemen). I had two younger sisters and a talent for getting into trouble. My parents were less than thrilled when the Catholic elementary school I attended suggested a smart-aleck kid like me would be better off in public school. (I was not considered "college material".) Sister Mary Frances should only see me now!

I loved public school! I loved the freedom and independence. I loved math and gym. I loved the extra free time I had to watch my favorite TV programs like "Superman" and "Abbott and Costello." So many of those old black and white adventure series and comedies centered around newspaper offices or radio broadcasts. I was fascinated. But I didn't aspire to be Jimmy Olsen or even Clark Kent. I wanted to be Perry White. I wanted to be in charge of the whole thing! I didn't realize it then, but I wanted to be even a step beyond Perry White: I wanted to *own* that "great metropolitan newspaper."

In other words, I had the authentic American Dream: I wanted to run my own business.

And so, at the age of ten, I started a shoeshine business. I put together a cardboard box and a couple of cans of Shinola, and every nice day after school I'd go down to the neighborhood bar and offer my services. I cleaned about ten pairs of shoes a day at ten cents a shine, but I made four times that much in tips because I was efficient, aggressive and cute. (The cute probably counted for a lot. Still does.) As I got older, my businesses got more complex, more time-consuming and more expensive to operate. I needed more money to live. In junior high I ran a lawn mowing service, by high school I had added a floor-polishing business, and in college (yes, I did go) I built my own hot dog concession.

After school I worked for a number of people doing everything from janitorial work to managing a disco to repairing appliances. I sold so many service contracts while fixing broken appliances that my boss suggested I concentrate on sales alone. Then I switched jobs and started selling insurance. From there it was a short jump to selling advertising. I was pretty good at selling ads for someone else, so I figured—why not try selling them for myself? I found my niche.

I envisioned a small magazine-like handout for nightclubs and restaurants, something that would encompass entertainment and leisure. It was in that germ of an idea that *Nightlife* was born. It was 1979, I was twenty-eight years old, and I was ready. Working out of my house, I pasted a dummy magazine together, sold ads at twenty-five dollars apiece, and in 1980 printed the first issue.

By mid–1980 I was three hundred thousand dollars in debt. I owed money to everyone I knew and a lot of people I didn't know. My wife was expecting our first baby, the bank was foreclosing on my house, and my luxurious executive office was a ten-by-ten-foot room in the basement of a funeral home. Now, little more than ten years later, I'm the chief executive officer of a multimillion-dollar business with three successful monthly magazines and a weekly entertainment update shown by cable TV networks throughout the country. How did I do it? The same way you can!

That's why I wrote this book.

Mike Cutino

## HOW TO FOCUS

*H*ow can common sense and timing work for you? There are four different stages you must learn to recognize and control.

The first is **focusing.** This includes awareness, evaluation and understanding. It includes using your head (common sense) and listening.

The second is **self-confidence.** This comes with positive thinking and feeling good about yourself.

The third is **timing,** the result of focusing and common sense.

The fourth is **imagination and effort**—going for it!

I will explain step-by-step how you can progress to achieve your goals and dreams—and succeed!

We use our five senses every day to make decisions

and to accomplish what we want to achieve. Some things we do automatically. We wake up, get out of bed, go into the bathroom, brush our·teeth. We don't *Focus* or think about these things. We automatically make our coffee and fix breakfast. We probably make a similar breakfast every working day because we have a routine and we function without considering alternatives.

Okay, we're in a rut. But if we ate breakfast in a different place every day—if we ate in the diner instead of at home, or if we ate at home instead of McDonald's —we'd have to think about choices. We'd order or make something different. For that day. And maybe the next.

Then we'd fall into a new routine and stop focusing once again.

Watch out. You may be in a "habit"—according to Webster, a state of body, natural or acquired: mode of growth: aptitude acquired by practice, custom, manner. It is strongly recommended that you analyze your positive and negative habits. A change is always good for the mind and body, and it could put you into a new frame of mind. For example, maybe you're getting up at nine o'clock and starting your workday at ten. If you change your nine o'clock wakeup habit to seven o'clock, this would give you more productivity and an added start for the day. It is very important to use all the resources possible to become successful. Why not? They are there for the taking!

Some things we have to do on automatic pilot. Not thinking about breakfast frees our mind for more important ideas. But—sometimes our whole life is on automatic pilot! We're in a comfortable (or maybe uncomfortable) rut and going nowhere. How do we change?

Sometimes it seems too overwhelming. You just don't know where to start, and you don't have the energy. That's probably why you picked up this book. You're not quite satisfied with where you are now and you're looking for a quick and easy way to feel a little better.

Well, you've already taken the first step. By picking up this book, you have focused on the fact that you don't have everything exactly as you would like it.

## VISUALIZE

Your next step is to recognize what's worth changing. Visualize your ideal life. Go for the whole dream! How would you really like to be living? Where? With whom? Doing what?

Don't say it's impossible. Where there's a will, there's a way. Focus on that life, on that person you want to be. Keep the dream in mind and then think about the steps it would take to get you there. Write them down.

Don't be embarrassed to dream big. Things get accomplished step by step, not in one fell swoop. And dreams are the first step.

Suppose you're a secretary but you really want to be the next Madonna. Can you sing? Dream big, but be realistic about your talents and abilities. If you're a singing secretary, where do you start?

Sing everywhere! Join the church choir; join the community chorus. Volunteer to sing at weddings (and funerals). Join a theater group and audition for all the musicals. Make sure everyone you know knows about your talent and your wish to perform. If you have money, hire a voice coach. If you don't have money, find a coach and barter. Maybe you could babysit or clean the house or teach tennis in exchange for voice lessons. Go to the library and research music agents. Start putting yourself in the spotlight.

What have you got to lose? What if you really don't want to try because you could *fail!* And then everyone would know that you failed—and what would they say?

Failure. What does that mean? If you don't accomplish what you set out to do, you fail, right? Christopher Columbus set out to find a new route to India. Instead he discovered America. Did he fail? You bet! The guy did not do what he set out to do. And you may not, either. On your way to one goal, you may discover another. You may pocket the red ball instead of the blue. What you're doing is gaining experience. You're learning and changing and growing. We do not always go straight from A to B. Getting to B is not the problem. Getting off your A is!

Say you're a computer jock. You dream about playing major league baseball. But you're forty. You wish you were a teenager again; you wish you'd gone all out back then. But what can you do now? I'll tell you—so that when you're sixty, you won't be wishing you were forty and could make a move.

Get off your A: Assess your talents and make a list of all the ways you could be involved in major league baseball using the computer skills you now have. Research job opportunities connected with major leagues and stadiums. Decide whether you really want to/need to relocate to get yourself involved in the sports world. Call every sports freak and jock friend you know looking for leads and connections.

No one can possibly help you achieve your goal if it's a secret daydream! You have to decide what's really important and what isn't, what's a real goal and what's a fantasy. Then *move* on it.

Walt Disney did not grow up with the vision of creating Disneyland. He was a poor kid who got up at 4:30 in the morning so he could get his newspapers delivered before school started. He lived in a small four-room apartment in Kansas City with his parents and four brothers and sisters.

Times were tough. If there was ever any extra money, Walt would escape to the vaudeville shows or go watch the new "motion" pictures. He used the little free time he had to draw and doodle and perform funny skits to amuse his little sister.

By the time he was in high school, he knew what he was going to do with his life—he was going to be a political cartoonist with one of the city newspapers. So he drew for his high school paper. He did caricatures of the patrons at the neighborhood barber shop. He even managed to study art three nights a week while he was going to high school *and* working as a handyman in a jelly factory.

But World War I interfered with Disney's dreams of a hotshot newspaper job in Kansas. While he was still seventeen, he found himself in France serving with the American Ambulance Corps. He continued sketching satirical cartoons, and when he returned to the States, he made the rounds of all the local newspaper offices.

No one was impressed. But Disney persisted in trying to find a job where he could draw, and finally he was hired for fifty dollars a month as an apprentice to two commercial artists. His job was to draw rough drafts of ads for farm supplies—a far cry from Mickey Mouse!

But Disney was energetic and eager, and his whimsical flair paid off. He was promoted to doing the artwork for weekly theater programs. The dream to draw and to get paid for it was still alive and well. It just wasn't working out exactly the way he had envisioned it.

Milton Hershey's story is similar. He certainly didn't dream of owning a chocolate empire. In fact, when he was a child during Civil War days, chocolate was not a familiar candy. Ice cream was the big treat of the time, and caramels were the candy in demand.

Hershey's childhood dream was to move back to his original family home in Pennsylvania (now known as Hershey, Pennsylvania). His father was a jack-of-all-trades, master-of-none who had managed to lose the family farm and move his family three times before Hershey started school. And even though he was just a little kid, Hershey knew that to get back to that first house he'd lived in, he'd need money. At the mature age of six, whenever he could sneak away from home, he'd gather the coal which had spilled along the railroad track and sell it to the townspeople for a penny a pailful.

Eventually his parents discovered his entrepreneurship, and it influenced their decision to return to the community where Milton was born. Obviously his hard work and single-minded focus had paid off. He learned that lesson early and never forgot it.

When he was twelve, he was apprenticed to a printer. Even though Milton was a hard worker and possessed a great curiosity about the world around him, he was adolescently clumsy and not particularly fond of scholarly pursuits. He hated the printing trade. But because his parents had invested good money in this opportunity for him, he heeded his mother's favorite maxim: "A Hershey never quits."

Unfortunately (or perhaps for candy lovers, fortunately), Hershey didn't have to quit. After knocking over a whole tray of type, then losing his hat in the press (which immediately jammed up), Milton was curtly dismissed.

After this failure, Milton's mother found her son an apprenticeship with Joseph Royner, Lancaster's leading confectioner and ice cream maker. Hershey loved it; this was exactly what he wanted to do! He spent four years learning about mixing and flavoring, cleanliness and honesty. He was such a good worker, doing more than he was ever asked, anticipating needs, experimenting with new ideas, that his boss expressed his admiration for Milton by naming his own first-born son Milton also. Hershey was not only flattered, but determined not to disappoint his teacher and friend.

He was going to strike out on his own and become the best caramel maker around.

When I was in junior high school, I started a lawn mowing business. I didn't want to work for anyone else. I wanted to be in charge. I also had no intention of sharing my profits. By the end of my first summer, I had fifteen regular clients.

Unfortunately, you can't mow grass on Long Island in the winter. I had to think of an indoor money-making business I could do after school and on weekends. Somehow it came to me that people who are fussy about their outdoor grounds would be equally fussy in the winter about their indoor grounds—i.e., their floors. I decided to start a floor-waxing business. With the money I'd saved from cutting grass, and a loan from my parents, I bought the equipment I needed. I didn't drive yet, so my parents drove me and my polisher to my weekly jobs. I charged a dollar a floor. It only cost me about twenty-five cents in overhead, plus my time, and of course, I had to wax my parents' floors for free. The floor waxing became a year-round business and I made money all through high school.

When I graduated, my uncle got me into the electrical workers' union in New York City. I was going to make $2.15 an hour that summer, and all I had to do was lug steel cable up fifty flights of steps.

That first exhausting day, I went outside on my lunch break and bought a hot dog from the guy on the corner. As I stood leaning against the building resting up for the afternoon, I counted how many people bought hot dogs. In one hour, he had over sixty-five customers—more than one a minute! I decided then and there to go into the hot dog business.

The first thing I did was build a hot dog stand. It cost me about eighty dollars in materials and I sold it for three hundred dollars. I built a second one and sold that for four hundred dollars. With my profits, I bought a professional hot dog cart and made money all through college selling hot dogs.

When I was through with the cart, I sold it to a local disco. The kid who ran the concession stand there didn't pay attention to what he was doing, and the cart caught fire. The disco owners called me up to see if I could fix it for them, and while I was working on that, the janitor was having a hard time with the floor polisher. So I fixed that, too, and showed him how to properly polish a floor.

The disco owners were so impressed, they fired the janitor and hired me to clean the place during the day and manage the concessions at night. As a bonus, they gave me back my hot dog stand!

The common thread in these three stories is that neither Disney nor Hershey nor I set out specifically to become what we became. We focused on the opportunities presented to us. We worked hard with what we had. And we never stopped expanding. There are lots of steps between what you think you want to do, what you are doing, and where you eventually end up. Where you end up could be the beginning of something new.

One of the problems today is that we're all in a rush to complete and do everything as soon as possible. We always have sixteen things that had to be done yesterday. We have to stop and take stock of what is going on.

*Focusing* is the ability to zero in on one specific target.

For example, imagine you're at the rifle range competing with an expert marksman. There are ten bull's-eyes to hit, and you have fifty bullets. Your fifty are in a machine gun. When you press the trigger, the bullets whizz out, one after another. Chances are you'll hit two or three or maybe even half the bull's-eyes because of the sheer quantity of bullets. But the expert marksman chooses an appropriate weapon and carefully aims one shot at a time. And hits them all.

On a clear day, you can see forever. On a foggy day, you can't. Consequently, on a foggy day you focus much better. You really have to look to see where you're going. Treat your life like a foggy day. Be aware and concentrate on every step. Don't trip over branches. If you're sure-footed in the fog, just think how quick you'll be when a clear day comes!

Remember that focusing is fine-tuning, whether you are focusing a camera, a television, binoculars, a microscope, a telescope, or your awareness. Focusing is turning your attention to a specific object or situation and seeing it clearly, seeing it as if for the first time.

What we are familiar with, we don't see anymore. We don't notice our children growing unless we haven't seen them for a while. We don't notice all the spring buds until they burst into flowers. And while our lack of attention isn't necessarily detrimental—I mean, just how much can one absorb?—it is important to retain the ability to focus, to scan with an objective eye, not only to see, but to define. And not only to define, but to decide.

I want you to pay attention to everyone you talk to today. Listen to them. That's why God gave us two ears and only one mouth! Do not pay half attention. Look at the person, and I mean in the eye. Focus all your attention on that person and what he or she is saying. Blank out the rest of the world. Do you understand what is being said?

When people speak, they are trying to relate a central idea. Do you clearly understand what they are saying? If you're not sure, ask. Ask them to simplify it for you or to give you an example. You have to listen carefully when someone speaks to you. Stop what you're doing and focus on what is being said. Is unloading the dishwasher really more important than focusing on your child? Is listening to the news really more important than listening to another person?

Your biggest and most effective power in communication is listening. When you don't know what to say, listen. Don't just speak for the sake of speaking. If a person wants to argue and you don't respond, you get your point across much more effectively than if you fire back a lot of angry words. By listening, and just by listening, you can sometimes sway the odds in your favor. The speaker doesn't know for certain if you're bored, angry, confused, or if you fully understand. Once you open your mouth, you define your position.

If I were President of the United States, I would introduce a new subject into our school systems:

*LISTENING.* I would make it mandatory for all students to take this course. A trained ear can give you a communication edge.

If you are able to focus on what is being said to you, a number of things will start happening.

First, the person you have focused on will realize they have your full attention. It will make them feel worthwhile and it will make them feel trusting. When someone trusts you, you feel more responsible. Responsible people get more done. They succeed more. (How many irresponsible successes do you know?)

Second, once you start really listening, you hear more. You become aware of tone, modulation, emotion. You begin to tune into what is really going on, not just what is being said. You begin to focus on motives and actions. Your awareness expands, and with it, your knowledge. Once you start focusing, you start analyzing people, problems, situations. You become aware of more than one answer.

Sometimes there are several options. Focusing helps you think. If you can define a problem, it is easier to find a solution. You have to remember that most problems often have more than one solution. There isn't one right answer. If the front door is locked and you don't have a key, you have to go through the back door. And if the back door is locked, you have to go through a window. Sometimes that unlocked window is in the basement, and sometimes it's on the second story; then you have to get a ladder or climb a tree to get to it. Sometimes all the doors and windows are locked. What do you do then? Sometimes you break in.

Sometimes you call the police. Sometimes you wait for someone else who has a key. There is always more than one solution to a problem. You must keep that in mind.

Focusing on an individual is very important. You'll learn to analyze that person and understand their strengths and weaknesses. Always focus on their strengths. Appeal to them. Use them. Let people know that you recognize their capabilities and depend on them.

Am I saying use people? Absolutely. Use the best they have to offer and let them know it. Appreciate them! They'll never let you down. How do you feel when someone asks you to do something for them? Appreciated.

And how do you feel once you've done the favor and they barely say thank you? You don't like it! In fact, you probably decide that that's the last time you'll ever go out of your way for so-and-so.

But think how you feel when you do something for someone and your efforts are positively remarked upon and appreciated. You feel good. You'd be happy to help them again. You know they respect and value your help. And you work harder to justify their expectations.

Trust begets trust and doubt begets doubt. That's COMMON SENSE. Sometimes if you are told you might not succeed, you work extra hard to prove that premise wrong. But more often, you don't work as hard as you might because an expectation of failure already exists.

# FOCUS ON THE POSITIVE

You cannot change yourself or the people around you overnight, but you can start right now. When your mother said, "If you can't say anything nice, don't say anything at all," she was right. Learn to bite your tongue! Focus on what you are saying and how you say it.

For example, let's say you took a trip to the Bahamas for a week. You had a beautiful vacation, wonderful weather, excellent hotel accommodations, fantastic food. It was a terrific getaway. But when you flew back, the plane ride was awful. It was the worst flight you've ever been on and, what's more, your luggage was lost.

The next day, a friend inquires about your vacation. Do you say your vacation was fine and then focus on all the miserable details of your horrible airline fiasco, or do you answer the question about your vacation and tell them how absolutely marvelous the Bahamas were? Do you leave your friend with a negative impression of your trip (so he's sorry he even asked) or a positive outlook (so maybe he'll vacation there himself)?

But what if your vacation truly *was* terrible? You can still describe it in a way that you and your friend can laugh about it. Think of a situation that recently took place in your life that you described negatively. Reevaluate it. Can you get your point across in a positive way? Suppose you went to the beach. It was 85 degrees, sunny and gorgeous. But at four o'clock, a storm blew in and it poured. When your coworker asks the next day, "How was the beach?" how do you respond?

You can say, "Well, we were having a great time, but then it poured. I got soaked to the skin. My hat was ruined. What a lousy day." You could just as easily have said: "It was a beautiful day. The weather was great. There were lots of people—and to top it off, there was a downpour about four o'clock. You should have seen everybody scrambling to get out of the rain. It was so funny!" Now you've taken the idea of having a terrible time because it rained and transformed it into a continuation of a good time because it rained.

People want to share good times with you. Common sense tells you nobody wants to share bad times.

Try to relate your trying times as amusing adventures. Or don't mention them at all. We all gravitate toward positive people, to those whose cups are half full, not half empty.

The fact that you had a flat tire on your way to the airport and missed your flight to Chicago for an important two o'clock presentation is only a tragedy if you present it as such.

If you constantly complain about your problems, you will be perceived as a negative, incompetent person. Somehow things always go wrong for you; you lead a life of excuses. You have to put your problems into perspective. Having a flat tire and missing your flight could make a very amusing story. You'd laugh if you saw it on "Cosby." You must have looked pretty funny in your good clothes stuck on the parkway without a spare! How did you ever get out of that jam? What happened to the people waiting in Chicago? Did you lose thousands of dollars and was your life ruined forever? Or were you only inconvenienced?

Having a positive view of things makes adapting to life's unanticipated quirks much easier.

Remember, things can *always* be worse! By putting your tire problem into perspective, you can focus on the *important* things in your life.

## FOCUS ON THE IMPORTANT THINGS

Just what are the important things in your life? After the necessities are taken care of, what is your life about? What is important to you?

Consider the possibilities. Are your children important? Your spouse? Your family? Your dog? Your job? Your boat? Your house? Are your ideals important? Your morals? Your religion? Your political philosophy? Is making money important to you? What do you do with your time? How do you fill your day? If you had more time, what would you be doing with it?

Part of the process of focusing is tuning into your own needs and wants. If you can't be honest with yourself here, you have no chance of achieving a sense of control, of self-confidence. *You* are in charge of how you use your time. The choices are all yours.

Don't say your marriage is most important if you spend most of your time at work under the guise of supporting your family. You're kidding yourself. You're spending all your time working because that's where you feel good, that's where your ego gets stroked, and maybe that's where you're escaping from your family.

Don't say your job is most important if you take off as much time as possible and daydream away the hours you are at work. Obviously you don't want to be there. You're unhappy with your work and escaping from it as often as you can. Focus on why. Is it the kind of job, the atmosphere, the boss, the boredom? What kind of job would hold your attention? Do you really want a job at all?

It's hard to be honest with yourself, but you can't begin to know what you want or where you're going if you are saying one thing and doing another. You have to know who you are and what you want. Not what your mother wants for you, or your spouse, or your best friend. What do *you* want?

When you know what is important to you, when you listen to your inner self, when you understand that you are in control of *your life,* you can begin to make things work for you. Common sense tells you you can't feel good about yourself if you're living a lie. Productivity is directly proportionate to self-confidence. Achievers keep achieving.


## POSITIVE ATTRACTS POSITIVE


How does a loser become a winner? How do you change the cycle? First, you have to want to change.

Start by focusing on yourself and how you're treating others. Change your negative outlook to a positive one. Self-control is important. You can train your mind to think a certain way. You can reprogram yourself! You won't turn into an optimist overnight, but once you try to control your attitude, you will become more and more positive. And positive attracts positive.

Don't be on the defensive all the time. You usually don't win a chess game by playing defensively. Be aggressive. Don't get backed into a corner. But know when to quit. There's a lot to be said for persistence, but you have to know when an effort is fruitless. Don't back away from problems, but be sure you've focused *on the problem*. Sometimes we make assumptions when we should be asking for facts. Be aware of what's happening around you. Ask questions. Listen. Listen to yourself.

And remember it's those foggy days, the times when you don't know where you're heading or what the next step will bring, that are your *opportunity* to focus most intensely on those problems. If you can focus when times are troubled, think how poised you'll be when things are going well for you!

*Think self-confidence.*

# BE
# SELF-CONFIDENT

*S*ome people seem to be born with self-confidence. They always know what to say. They always look good. They succeed at what they try to do. How come? What is it about them?

First of all, they work at it. Sometimes what seems effortless has taken years of trial and error.

And second, they believe in themselves. They don't expect to do poorly. They persist until they master whatever they're trying to do.

Remember, there are no overnight successes. There are no "instant winners."

When you read newspaper articles about people who've won tons of money in a lottery, have any of them been first-time players? No! Read on and you'll find that they buy ten tickets a week, that they've been playing the same numbers for three years. They have been persistent.

Anything you do is like that lottery, whether we're talking grades or jobs or even looking good. You can help weigh the odds in your favor, but you have to try to succeed.

Successful people usually focus on the positive. When you talk to them, you hear all sorts of good things, but you don't hear the gripes, fears and uncertainties. You don't hear about what they didn't do; you hear about what they *did* do. These are interesting people. They *do* things.

What do you say when you come from work and your spouse says, "Hi honey! How was your day?" Do you launch into an amusing story of the day's events or perfunctorily reply, "The usual"? Are you guilty of one-word responses? What a boring life you lead!

Didn't anything happen to you at all today? What did you do for those eight hours? You know, if your life isn't interesting to you, it won't be of interest to anyone else either.

You must make an effort to move toward a positive self-image, both in how you look and what you say. Remember: you are unique! There is no one else exactly like you in the whole world! You are *one-of-a-kind!*

That doesn't mean you're perfect just the way you are. It doesn't mean you can't be improved. Everyone needs to keep learning, growing, changing. You *can* be what you want to be. But not overnight—and not without effort. And only you can be you—you're starting out by being special.

How do you get self-confidence? Where do you begin? Wouldn't it be easy if you could just go buy some? Put it on your MasterCard!

Self-confidence, like charity, begins at home. Or in this case, with you, your image, your body.

The first step to being self-confident (successful) is *looking* confident (successful).

When you like the way you look, you feel good. You feel secure, comfortable, confident. You feel capable. And you *are* capable. You are capable because you have the ability to make yourself look good. And once you are able to do that, you are ready to do a lot more.

How do successful people look? Are they sloppy, dirty, droopy, thrown together? Do they look like they grabbed whatever was lying on the closet floor?

Of course not. They look clean, neat. They look unfrazzled. They look *in control,* even when they're out of sorts.

You can look that way too. You are what you wear in today's society. It goes a lot further than just not wearing jeans when you go for a job interview. There are books devoted to teaching you how to dress. But before you even consider what to wear, take a look at the body your clothes are going on. Look at each day as a new beginning, a fresh start.

The best place to start fresh is in the shower. As you shampoo your hair, focus on your plans for the day. Think about one specific thing you are going to accomplish, your main goal for the day. It doesn't have to be signing a million-dollar account. It can be as simple as organizing all the papers on your desk or phoning four people you haven't had time for. Don't think about the impossible when planning a daily goal. Think about what you *can* do today as a positive step toward that "impossible" dream. Imagine doing whatever your chosen task is. Think about how good you're going to feel to get it taken care of. Use your shower time to groom for success!

Clean hair is good, but when was the last time you had it cut, styled or shaped? Are you wearing your hair the same way you did in your high-school yearbook? That's okay if you're still in high school.

If you're not, it's time for a change. A haircut is an inexpensive investment in a successful new you.

When you're getting your hair cut, make an appointment for the next time. If you have an appointment scheduled, you'll go. If you don't plan appointments, you'll be looking shaggy before you get around to it again.

It's a fact that most successful businessmen do not have facial hair. Beards and mustaches proliferate in the more creative or academic professions. Presidents, politicians and power people, in general, are clean-shaven.

What about your weight; or, how overweight is overweight? If your size is a consideration, you have to decide what to do about it. But your weight is not an excuse for poor grooming and sloppy dressing. Indeed, since by your very size you are more noticeable, you should take care to be more presentable.

When's the last time you saw your dentist? If you haven't had a checkup in over a year, make an appointment right now. Haven't you noticed that successful people smile a lot? (They have a lot to smile about.)

I won't presume to tell you women how to put on makeup. You can take advantage of those free makeovers major department stores are always promoting. You can take books out of the library to learn how to apply makeup the most effective way. Most fashion magazines have articles on various ways of using cosmetics.

You don't have to spend a lot of money to look successful. A knowledgeable woman will look as good in makeup from Woolworth's as she will with France's most expensive export. The key word here is *KNOWL-EDGE*. It's important to talk to the experts. Cosmeticians are trained to match the right colors to your skin tones. They know how to minimize imperfections and maximize your best features.

Call me a male chauvinist, but professional women look better in skirts than in pants. A well-cut, two-piece suit is always acceptable. Dresses in simple classic styles, in solid neutrals, primary colors, or conservative prints, are also attractive. Common sense will tell you that hot pink and chartreuse are not colors you wear in a professional situation if you expect to be taken seriously.

Avoid big dangling earrings and clunky bracelets or rings. Stick with small gold or pearl earrings. Save your diamonds for after hours. The image you want to project is one of self-assurance and competence.

Men must decide whether to wear a three-piece suit, a two-piece suit or a sports jacket and slacks. Sometimes a two-piece suit breaks up the monotony of a business meeting where everyone looks alike wearing three-piece suits.

On the other hand if you aren't dressed like everyone else, do you have enough self-confidence to handle it?

Suit dressing is a bit like putting on a uniform. Sometimes we have to conform so we can be heard. You don't want your suit to be louder than you. Stick to dark blue or gray, and remember, if you're over-dressed, you can always undress. If you arrive at a meeting in your three-piece and it's two-piece event, get rid of the vest. If it's even more casual, loosen your tie or take off your jacket. Roll up your shirt-sleeves.

The key is adaptability. Never be more dressed or better dressed than your boss—unless you want his job!

Ties are very important and so is the way you tie your knot. Clip-on ties indicate laziness and lack of attention to detail. As for tie color, make sure you have a few red ties or ties with red accents in your collection. Red is a classic power color. Save those pastel and madras ties for summer casual wear. Be conservative in your choice of colors. It's your thoughts and ideas you want noticed, not your ties.

It takes a lot of time and money to put together a good-looking, conservative and stylish business wardrobe. You have to make the decision that you are going to invest time and money in making yourself look good. Investing in yourself will definitely pay off ten times over.

The motion picture industry spends millions of dollars each year for someone to coordinate clothing to characters and plot. The next time you watch television or go to a movie, focus on the clothing the characters are wearing. Look at their hair and makeup. A lot of thought has gone into how the actors look, how they're dressed. Even though you probably can't remember what anyone wore in the last film you saw (unless it was *Gone With the Wind*), the appropriateness of their clothing highlighted the story, which you do remember. And just like this example, you want people to remember you and what you had to say rather than remembering what you wore.

Planning is essential for looking good. Decide what to wear the night before. That gives you time to make sure everything is clean and pressed, and to see that all buttons and hems are intact. Decide what accessories you'll be wearing and what shoes. If you get into a night-before habit, you will not be frantically searching for a needle or standing indecisively before your closet. The next morning you will start the day in control of yourself. The morning will begin calmly and efficiently. This is the beginning of a positive day!

Before you put your best foot forward, take a look at the hand you'll be extending to greet the new boss or close the deal.

Are you still a nail-biter? Nail-biting in an adult is like thumb-sucking in a baby. If you're guilty of this one, you *must* stop. Most people bite their nails because they are nervous or anxious about something, and they are not at ease in a given situation. If you don't care about the details of how you look, how can I believe you'll care about the details of handling my account?

Many of us seem to feel a need to keep our mouths busy even when we're not talking. We can't just keep our hands in our laps or on the desk. If our hands are not traveling back and forth to our mouths, they occupy themselves on other parts of our head. We are hair-twirlers, beard-strokers, glasses-pushers, nose-scratchers, hair-patters, eye-rubbers, ear-pullers, head-scratchers, earring-fixers, and neck-massagers.

Most of these are unconscious habits; we're not even aware we're doing them. Try to focus on where you put your hands today. Watch others. There's the tie-straightener, the necklace-twirler, the ring-twirler, the fingernail-inspector, the nail-polish-remover, the knee-stroker, and the pen-tapper. These people are not in control of their bodies. Their bodies are controlling them.

When you're fidgeting, you aren't totally focused on the person you're trying to communicate with. Subliminally they'll recognize your distraction. Try to uncover your own particular quirky habits and consciously work to avoid them. In essence, reprogram yourself. Eliminate the unnecessary. Take control. Keep your hands and body in repose and your eyes and mind alert.

# BREAK THE "STUBBORN" HABIT

Do you know the kind of person who can never accept or take blame for anything? If something doesn't go their way, they try to find an excuse to blame their misfortunes on someone else. Perhaps they're too stubborn to try a new approach. Is that you? How do people view you? How do they react to you? It's difficult to be objective about ourselves, but sometimes we need to take off our rose-colored glasses and find those faults which are holding us back. We can't correct something that we don't recognize.

Some people are too stubborn to say "yes" to a great opportunity. They want to be coaxed. Some people are always trying to impress someone else or make someone else happy. They never realize what would make them happy. These people are actually being stubborn about their own happiness!

And being stubborn is being stupid. The one who suffers for it is the person who doesn't recognize the problem because he's afraid he'll fail: he has no self-confidence.

People are stubborn because they are scared: they don't want to try, they don't want to make an effort. What a lack of common sense! In my survey, sixteen percent of the people said they were extremely stubborn and the same sixteen percent wished they could control it. Sometimes we are so bogged down in a behavior problem that we need some professional help. But often, if we recognize our problem, we can change our responses ourselves. The person who understands that he has a stubborn streak can learn to control it.

When you are presented with an opportunity, think for a minute if you will benefit from it, learn from it, get something out of it. If you will, say yes. Take the chance. Take the risk. You have to start moving in a positive direction. And it will get easier as you get used to being more agreeable. You'll begin to break that stubborn habit. You'll make others around you happy. And positive feelings are contagious!

## MAKING FANTASIES REAL

Once we become aware of our own shortcomings and are working towards control of our own personal environment, the next step is to evaluate our position in the game plan of life. How do we progress from A to B? Where does the dream stop and the reality begin?

We all give in to fantasy, but all dreams have their roots in reality. There is a germ of possibility in every fantasy we have. Sometimes you have to take pen and paper in hand and seriously list the steps you see to move from one stage to the next.

Even though it may seem silly to try this exercise:

Take your fondest, most impossible dream. Write it down. The translation from thought to actual black and white will help define your goals. Be as detailed as possible. List all the obstacles in your way.

Now list as many ways as you can think of to get around these obstacles. Don't look for practical solutions. The sky is always the limit. A crazy idea may springboard you to a practical solution.

Self-confident people make plans for their future. They don't just wait to see what happens.

When Walt Disney got his first drawing job with the commercial artists, he met another eighteen-year-old, Ub Iwerks, who did lettering and airbrushing. The two become close friends, and when they were let go from their jobs (due to a lack of work), they decided to open their own business.

They didn't have any money, but they had a lot of ideas and a lot of self-confidence. They made an agreement with a friend for two desks and office space in exchange for doing some design work.

They were in business for about a month (and making more money than they previously had) when the Kansas City Slide Company advertised for a cartoonist. Ub understood this was what Walt really wanted to be doing, and urged him to apply for the job. This slide company hired Disney for forty dollars a week and a few months later, on Disney's recommendation, they hired Iwerks too.

The company soon changed its name to Film Ad because they made one-minute advertising cartoons that were shown in motion picture theaters. Disney was fascinated with the idea of cartoons that moved, and he was certain he could create even better ones. He researched all he could on animation and motion and, with Iwerks, began re-drawing the existing cartoons. The team started interjecting their own punchlines, and the company liked them.

But Disney wasn't content limited to one-minute ads. He began experimenting on his own, and, with a borrowed camera, put together three hundred feet of cartoon which he took to a local theater. The manager liked it and asked for one a week!

So Disney worked for Film Ad by day and for himself at night, making the cartoon shorts he called Laugh-O-Grams. He suggested to his bosses at Film Ad that they might consider expanding to short cartoons, but they weren't interested. So Disney decided to make them on his own.

His first idea was to do a series of animated fairy tales. He advertised for apprentice cartoonists and bartered with them, offering instruction instead of wages, and promising a share in whatever profits would be made.

After six months of evening work, their first production, a seven-minute *Little Red Riding Hood*, was ready. Disney thought it was so terrific he quit his job at Film Ad and, with fifteen thousand dollars from several small investors, he launched his own company, Laugh-O-Gram Films. Iwerks left Film Ad to join him. They found a distributor in New York and made a six-cartoon deal for nine thousand dollars!

But Disney didn't stop there. He tried doing newsreels. He filmed babies and children for parents (with private home showings). He even made the forerunner of the music video for a music company.

Unfortunately, the film distributor in New York went out of business without ever paying Laugh-O-

Gram Films. Disney's funds were dwindling. His staff quit. Iwerks returned to his old job. Disney couldn't afford the rent on his apartment, so he moved into the office (the rent had been paid there well in advance). He ran a tab at the local cafe and took baths at the railroad station.

One day Disney received a call from a prospective client, and he couldn't go meet him because his only pair of shoes were being repaired and Disney didn't have the dollar and a half to pay for them. Talk about hard times!

The understanding client, a local dentist, gave Disney the money to retrieve his shoes and hired him to produce a five-hundred-dollar cartoon on dental health.

Working always inspired Disney to new creative efforts, and he came up with the idea of putting a real person into an animated world. He sent several letters to film distributors describing his new concept for *Alice in Wonderland*. But before he was done with the film, he was broke. He managed to finish the work, but his investors were reluctant to put up any more money.

So, at the age of twenty-two, Disney declared Laugh-O-Gram Films bankrupt, packed his bag— and headed for Hollywood! . . . Talk about self-confidence . . .

Milton Hershey did much the same thing. After his apprenticeship in the confectioner's shop, it was time to strike out on his own. He had saved fifty dollars and his Aunt Mattie gave him a starter loan of one hundred and fifty dollars. It was 1876, the year of the Great Centennial Exposition in Philadelphia. What better place to open his first candy store?

Milton, not quite twenty, started a little storefront shop specializing in taffy and caramels. Since he couldn't afford space inside the Exposition, he stationed himself outside the main gates every day with his pushcart of fresh candies.

He was a great success: indeed, he had more business than he could handle by himself, so his mother and his nephew and a friend, Lebbie, came to help him. Within a year, they had to move to bigger quarters.

But even though the business was expanding, the penny candies did not bring in enough money to pay the high sugar bills. Milton had to ask his aunt for another loan. This was the beginning of a series of family loans, for as the business grew, the debts grew. Hershey was working eighteen to twenty hours a day to stay ahead of the orders. His aunt came to work with him, and even his father turned up.

It was just too much. By December 1881, Hershey had collapsed from stress and exhaustion. He was laid up for two months. And even though his mother and aunt tried to run the shop, his business failed and he was forced to close his doors.

Disappointed, but not discouraged (there *is* a difference), Hershey decided to head west and try candy-making in Denver. He didn't have the money to set up his own business, and he was smart enough to realize that no prospective employer would hire him if they knew he was an aspiring competitor. So Hershey hired on as a candymaker as if he were just fresh from his apprenticeship—and he learned a whole new aspect of the business!

In the West, there weren't candy stores or push-carts that people frequented daily. The candy made in town was usually delivered to outlying mining camps and ranches. Often it had to be transported for several days. Therefore, the candy had to be made so it would taste fresh and not spoil.

The Denver confectioner's secret was milk. And from that time on, it would be one of Hershey's ingredients too. He had learned a basic Life Rule: You Can Always Learn More.

After he had learned all the Denver job could offer him, Hershey set off for Chicago, where his father was trying to establish a carpentry business, and again attempted to set up in candy-making, but within three months they were both broke and heading for New Orleans. They managed to survive in New Orleans for only five months.

Hershey was finding that his two biggest problems in the candy business were getting credit and obtaining the constant supply of sugar he needed. He had not yet figured out how to run a business. Obviously, hard work alone was not enough.

But despite his string of failures, Milton Hershey had optimism. He *knew* he was a remarkable confectioner, and that he would eventually succeed. So he decided to try his luck in the toughest market in the world—New York City.


## FOLLOW YOUR HEART


Call it confidence, call it chutzpah, call it crazy— whatever you want to name it, it's one of the major ingredients of success. It is that ability to continue, to persevere, and to follow your heart when the odds seem insurmountable.

Both Disney and Hershey experienced failures and setbacks. They lost money. They went deep into debt. They worked till they dropped. And still they kept at it. They didn't consider chucking it all for a steady paycheck and safe jobs. Their minds were too focused and their visions too certain for that. They knew where they wanted to go and what they wanted to do. They tried and they kept on trying. And you can, too.

When you see clearly the goal you want, you can plan step by step how you're going to get there. Every day you can do something, learn something, talk to someone, to help move closer to your dream. Once you make a decision, stand by it. Follow through. Don't be afraid to take the ball and run with it. And don't be afraid to fall down. You can always get up and get running again.

Different decisions bring different rewards. Often we dismiss the experience we gain from an unwise choice when in reality we've won a bit of wisdom. Perhaps the choice wasn't bad, but the timing was. We have to constantly reevaluate what's behind us while we decisively move ahead. Reevaluating a position does not mean waffling. It means looking at all the angles. Sometimes it means making new decisions.

For example, you have decided to leave the firm of Peach, Pear & Apple to join Pickle, Pepper & Plum. As usually happens after we resolve to make a change, something unexpected and unanticipated occurs. Peach, Pear & Apple offer you a comfortable promotion with an opportunity to expand your talents.

Do you immediately rescind your plan to leave? No. You reevaluate the plan. You now have more information to consider. You may decide not to leave after you have reevaluated your position. Or you may conclude that the promotion has come too late and decide to stick to your original decision.

Sometimes we make decisions with no pattern or goal in mind. We say yes to what sounds good at the moment. Often we're just flowing along with the current, doing the next thing that comes along. Successful people think about where they're going. They have a plan. You *have* to have one. Do you want to still be in the same place six months from now? A year? Five years?

Everyone wants to advance in some way. They want more money, more freedom, more status, more power, more time. No one is content with the status quo. No one is happy just getting by. Do you know anyone who says, "My life is perfect just the way it is. I wouldn't change a thing"? Of course not!

There isn't a person who has a problem-free life. No one has peace of mind. It is the one standard of success we will never totally grasp. And while we have glimmers of that ideal—all the bills are paid, our partners content, our houses clean, our bodies healthy and fit—we'll never achieve that state, even if we have millions and millions of dollars.

Anybody can make a lot of money. The problem

is: how are you going to keep it? When you accept that fact—that you will never be problem free—you can get on with the challenge of handling your life.

We often forget that living is survival. We get caught up in the quest for material goodies—I want a new CD player, I need a new VCR, I have to have a new car—and we lose touch with ourselves. Technologically we've evolved far from our cave-dwelling ancestors, but physically and emotionally we're still in the cave with them. We need food, shelter, warmth and companionship just as they did. And just like the cave-dweller, we need a plan of attack. How are we going to acquire these necessities? In this day and age, we forage and gather and hunt with money. We need money to buy the basics. But how do we get money? Sometimes it is given to us, some people steal it, but most people exchange work for money. That means we have to earn it.

There are all sorts of jobs, all kinds of "help wanted." You've never looked in the classified section of the paper and found no jobs available. There are hundreds of them, and they fall into two categories— simple and complicated. The simple ones pay little and any high school undergraduate can perform them. The complicated ones pay a lot more but require experience and training. The problem is: how do you get in the right position so you can be paid money for doing what you want to do?

First, you have to decide what you want. You have nothing to lose by trying. That's where step-by-step planning comes in. Second, take the courses you need.

Get the training. If you don't start some place, you'll never get anywhere. Third, put yourself in the right place. Be where the people are who do the sort of thing you want to do. You'll never learn to be a bullfighter if you stay in Tallahassee. Four, volunteer or work for peanuts to get the experience you need. Five, be persistent. Why take "no" for an answer, especially if it's not the answer you want? Perseverance usually pays off. That old axiom "if at first you don't succeed, try, try again" is one you should make part of your life.

Don't be shy about going after what you want. The worst that could happen is that you won't get it. The best that could happen is impossible to imagine.

With odds like that, what are you waiting for?

# TIMING COUNTS

*"It is circumstances and proper timing that give an action its character and make it either good or bad."*
— Agesilaus (444-360 B.C.)
*"Observe due measure, for right timing is in all things the most important factor."*
— Hesiod (ca. 800 B.C.)

*A*nimals have an instinctive sense of timing. Birds know when to build a nest, when to fly south, when to fly north. Bears know when to hibernate. Salmon rely on an instinctive sense of timing when they swim upstream to spawn.

Perhaps it is just a biological imperative, but the lower animals have an innate sense of timing and harmony that guides their lives. We have the same kinds of instincts. We know when it's time to eat; we take shelter when it's too cold or too hot; we rely on our senses to nurture and protect our bodies. But too often we don't continue that instinctive reliance when it comes to our careers or projects. We spend our time weighing pros and cons, looking at all the angles, imagining all the outcomes of any given action. We think too much! We are so busy debating possibilities that we often act too late. We hesitate.

Timing is a combination of instinct and intellect. When we toss all the combinations around, when we try to narrow the odds (whatever they might be), we're practicing. We're fine-tuning. This can be good. The problem arises when we never make the leap from preparation to performance. It's fine to consider all the outcomes that may develop from any major action we could take, but the bottom line is our knowing when to make our move—and then making it.

Athletes have a strong sense of timing. They develop it through practice. A boxer doesn't knock out his opponent because he gets lucky. He K.O.'s his rival because he sees the opportunity for an open shot and his "instinctive" (that is, *trained*) sense of timing acts on it. Bam!

When you see it, you've got to go for it. There may not be a second chance.

You've watched Olympic skaters. Every move is coordinated, every jump is planned. This is split-second timing. But they don't just put on their skates and win the gold. What you're seeing is the finished product after lots of planning and practice. Look at gymnasts. Perfect timing. They know where their bodies are. Again, it's planning and timing.

Where would trapeze artists be without timing? Or airplane pilots? Or your local pizza parlor? Imagine calling the pizzeria and ordering a pie with everything on it. You ask when it will be ready. The pizza man says he doesn't know. Doesn't he have a clock? Is he out of mozzarella? Is the oven broken? Is he backed up with forty orders? This is no way to run a business!

The problem with the pizza man is lack of planning and practice. To be successful, you have to have some idea of how long it will take to produce the finished product, whether you are making a pizza, or repairing a car, or publishing a book. It is very important to set a goal for yourself and a time limit to achieve that goal. Sometimes you'll misjudge the amount of time involved, but you can't leave a situation open-ended. You want to know *when!* And everyone you deal with wants to know *when* also.

## PLAN TOMORROW TODAY

Organization means knowing when. There is no way you can gain a sense of timing without getting yourself organized. You have to know where everything is, how to get information you don't have, who to ask, and what comes next. Start by making lists. Write everything down. Categorize it, classify it, file it into memory.

Everyone is a walking library of information.

Organized people know how to *retrieve and use* that knowledge. They know how much time is available to them and how they're going to use it. They can estimate how much time is involved in any project they undertake. This comes from planning and plain old common sense.

Do you know what you're going to be doing tomorrow? Do you have a calendar or appointment book? Take a look at it. How much do you have scheduled? What will you be doing at eleven o'clock? If you don't know, take ten minutes *now* and plan your day. Write down something for every hour. Don't just think about it. Don't just say, "Well, I'm going to the office, and then maybe I'll stop by the cleaners on my lunch hour, or I'll call Susie if I have a minute." Write down exactly what you intend to accomplish tomorrow. Write down what you're doing at work, what errands have to be done, and what time you're going to do them. Make yourself a schedule for one day, and then (this is the hard part) follow it! Do everything your list says to do. And cross off as you go.

At the end of the day, review your list. Did you get everything done? Did you misjudge your time? Carry over the undone things to the next day. Make a new list. Plan, plan, plan.

## DAYDREAM TIME

When you make this detailed plan, throw in some daydream time. At three o'clock you're going to take a coffee break; you're going to sit quietly at your desk and let your mind wander where it will. Plan to take fifteen minutes on your lunch hour just to sit in the park and look at the people. You have to give yourself leisure time. But you can plan it. Build the time into your schedule; otherwise your life is a series of unplanned days with some scheduled hours thrown in.

I know organization does not come easily to some people, but there is no way you're going to get ahead and reach that goal without making a plan. There is no way the pizza man will succeed if he doesn't know where he stored the cheese, if he doesn't have a recipe, and if he can't produce the pie on time.

What's true for the pizza man is true for you. You have to set your goal and plan how to get there. When you've made your lists and thought it out from several angles, you'll recognize when an opportunity arises that fits your possibilities, and you'll act on it. That's what timing is all about.


## TIMING CHANGES


Never be afraid of failure. If you think you failed, reevaluate the problem to see if you can find another solution. How else can you approach it?

Salespeople are often faced with rejection. For every client that says yes, eight or ten say no. If you consider every "no" a personal failure, you'll soon become a basket case. Learn not to take "no" personally.

Having a positive attitude is one of the important

secrets of success. You must always assume that the next person will say "yes." Here's where timing comes in. Just because Miss Scarlett said no on Tuesday doesn't mean she'll say no on Friday. Circumstances change. Timing changes.

Suppose you want to sell your car. You do your homework and you know it's worth six thousand dollars. You put an ad in the paper, and the next day someone offers you five thousand five hundred dollars. You probably say no. You think you can get six thousand dollars.

A month and a few low offers later, you still haven't sold your car. Payments are starting on the new car. Winter's coming. Someone again offers you five thousand five hundred dollars. This time you probably say yes. Why?

Circumstances.

Timing.

You've weighed the odds of getting six thousand dollars and reevaluated your position. Most often a no in business means "not at this time" as opposed to "not ever." So try, try, and try again.

Successful salespeople have merely mastered the art of timing. They don't take "no" personally. They've practiced enough to know when to ask and how to ask. And that means going through a lot of "no's."

## FOLLOW-UP

Remember, you have nothing to lose if someone says no and everything to gain if they say yes. So what if Professor Plum says he won't order a dozen Marvelous Murdering Mousetraps today. You didn't lose the sale. You just haven't made it—yet. If he ordered the mousetraps and then cancelled the order, you'd have lost the sale—maybe.

So next week you call the professor again to see if he could use the mousetraps. And when he says no, you send him more literature on why they are the best mousetraps ever made. And you call him again the next week.

By now you're either on a first-name basis or he's told you to get lost. But if you've been friendly, polite and helpful he won't be rude to you. He'll tell you no, but if he ever needs a mousetrap he'll call you. Put a star next to his name in the organized list of possibilities you have made. You don't have to call him every week, but stay in touch with him.

This is called follow-up. You did not take the original "no" for an answer. But if you ever expect to sell this man a mousetrap, you must stay in touch with him. Put him on your mailing list. Every three weeks, send him mousetrap memos. Someday this man will need a mousetrap or his friend will, and that's when he'll call you. But only if you've kept in contact. Otherwise, he'll go right to the Yellow Pages and forget all about you.

Follow-up is just as important as organization. It's as important when you get a yes as when you get a no.

Say Professor Plum bought ten mousetraps. Terrific! You made a nice commission. Thanks, Professor! Now what?

You call him the next week to thank him for the order. How are the mousetraps working out? Need any more? And a few weeks after that, you call again. Does he have any friends who need mousetraps? You put him on your mailing list and continue to send mouse memos.

A satisfied customer will tell his friends about you. Word of mouth can spread far and wide; it is the world's most effective advertising. And it doesn't cost you a cent.

See, you're making money already!

## SELLING YOURSELF

Sometimes follow-up means taking the mousetraps back. It means soothing upset clients and offering alternative solutions. If Mrs. Peacock cannot stand the sight of those dead mice, tell her straight out that your product is not for her. Use your common sense. She obviously needs a cat.

Then help her get one! Because what you are selling is not really mousetraps; what you're selling is yourself. And when Mrs. Peacock tells her garden club what a nice, helpful person you are, you'll get several orders for mousetraps (or cats).

I want to emphasize the significance of selling yourself. Everything we've been working toward so far has to do with the packaging and marketing of you and your ideas, from what you wear to how you speak to who you know.

You are organizing your *self*.

You are promoting your *self*.

And the reason you are doing all this is because you want something that you don't have now. Don't lose sight of that goal. What you are working toward is a new you—a more experienced you, a better you, a wealthier you. Keep visualizing yourself with whatever it is you want to accomplish. Remember, you're going to get there by using your common sense. You're planning, you're organizing, you're using every day to get closer to your dream.

## DON'T BE TOO REALISTIC

Even if your present goals are not realistic, someday they might be. This is where dreaming comes in.

When I say dreaming, I use the word loosely. For example, sometimes you watch a TV show like "Lifestyles of the Rich and Famous" and you daydream that one day you'll be in that position and they'll be interviewing you. And why not? It's possible. It's important when you set your goals that you also do a little dreaming. Plan for the short-term *and* the long-term.

Many people's dreams have become reality. Remember when lasers were only in science fiction stories? Remember the dream of man walking on the moon, or flying through the air? All these were fantasies once. Thomas Edison had dreams of making talking pictures. He tried and tried until he figured out a way to make the impossible possible. If you can dream it, you can *be* it eventually. Swindell wrote, "We are all faced with a series of great opportunities brilliantly disguised as impossible situations."

Alexander Graham Bell had a dream that people's voices could be heard at a distance, no matter how far. Now we have telephones not only in our houses, but in our cars, boats and planes. We have astronauts talking to us from outer space! Someone had a dream of flying faster than sound. Now we have the Concorde and can fly to Europe in a matter of hours.

Sometimes the offshoots of dreams are enormous. We used to go to the movies and say, gee I wish I could see that whenever I want to. Now we have VCRs and cablevision. Anything could be next!

Now, you may not have any startling inventions for mankind in mind. Maybe you just want to own your own home. Write down your goal and list all the possible ways to achieve it. The fastest way to get your own house is to buy what you want. That's another list—how to make money. Another approach to owning a house is to start by buying a piece of property that you will eventually build on. A third way is to start small and buy a cheap handyman's special which you can fix up and sell for a profit and invest again, moving up to the house of your dreams that way. A fourth way is to make an arrangement with a landlord to rent a house with the option of buying it, so that some of your rent money goes towards a down payment.

The odds of achieving your goal are now in your favor because you've considered several approaches. You might come across one of those possibilities when you least expect it, but because you've already considered it, your common sense will recognize the *time* to go for it! It's like making a flowchart. Have your goal on top and the different ways to achieve it on the bottom. Any time you come across one of those ways, you have to take that opportunity and make it work for you. Nobody else is going to do it for you. You must get going and do it yourself!

## MAKE THE FIRST MOVE

I want to share a story with you I know you will enjoy. Once you start to understand the theory of Common Sense and Timing, you will start to play with it, using it to help increase your success and your ability to advance yourself.

I'm the publisher of an entertainment magazine, *New York Nightlife*. I was under-capitalized from the very start. I had only four thousand five hundred dollars. Today it takes at least five million dollars to launch a magazine—and there is no guarantee that it will succeed. After two years of trying to wheel and deal, I had to do something to get the exposure necessary so people would be aware of my publication and buy it on the newsstand. I couldn't afford advertising on any radio station, let alone any of New York's top ten. I had to figure out how to get free radio advertising and, what's more, have it timed for when over-the-counter magazine sales were slow and when the advertising agencies were planning their next advertising budgets.

It seemed impossible. But nothing is impossible if you use your common sense and try to look at all the angles.

Everyone likes good press and favorable publicity. Radio personalities are no different; at least that's what I was hoping!

I did some research to find out who was the hottest disc jockey in New York. Then I contacted his radio station and told them I was going to do a cover story on them with a picture of their terrific DJ on the cover. When the disc jockey heard about this, he was thrilled. The station management was so ecstatic about the free publicity, they gave me carte blanche!

When my magazine came out, everyone was happy—especially the DJ, who announced all week long on the air that he was on the cover of *Nightlife*. He talked up my magazine so much that he was getting phone calls about it for two weeks.

There was no way I could put a price tag on the amount of free radio publicity I received. My total newsstand sales doubled! Advertising agencies heard and called to place advertising. And then I started receiving calls from other radio stations asking me to give the same exposure to their DJs!

I started trading radio time for advertising in my magazine. Not only was this a positive move for my business, it was a good move for the radio stations. An awareness of *Nightlife* was broadcast to over eight million listeners! I never could have afforded it! My forty-five-hundred dollar magazine is now valued at over six million dollars, and I've expanded to three other publications and two local TV shows.

The point to remember from my experience is that you can plan doing something good for yourself that also benefits others. You don't have to reveal all your reasons. If you make the first move, your "target" will be so flattered, he'll respond exactly as you want him to.

It's like playing tic-tac-toe. The guy who goes first always has control of the game. If you can master tic-tac-toe, you're on your way!

When Disney went off to Hollywood after his film company went bankrupt in Kansas, he made the rounds of the studios. He was hoping to get a job as a director (he always thought big), but there were no jobs available. He was finally hired as an extra in a cavalry scene.

This was not the way to make it in Hollywood! Disney realized that the only way he was going to get anywhere was with his cartoons. He fired off an impressive and self-confident letter to a previously encouraging New York film distributor, citing his relocation to the West Coast and enclosing a preview of the *Alice* film. In response, he received a telegram offering him a six-cartoon deal at fifteen-hundred dollars apiece.

Now that he had a commitment from New York, Walt was able to ask his brother, Roy, for backing, and together they formed Disney Brothers Studios. Disney contacted his old buddy Iwerks, and Ub came to Hollywood to work for Disney's new company.

The short films kept improving in quality and getting more expensive to produce. Disney always seemed to need just a little bit more money, but his work was beginning to be noticed favorably, and he was gathering a following. He signed another contract to produce eighteen more films in the *Alice* series at eighteen-hundred dollars per film, and the group moved to a new studio. With that move, they changed the name to Walt Disney Studios.

After two years of doing *Alice* films, it was time to move on to something else. Disney was getting bored. The founder of Universal Pictures suggested to the distributor that he'd like to see a cartoon series about a rabbit. *Oswald the Lucky Rabbit* became Disney's first all-animated cartoon.

When the original contract was up, Disney was confident that he could ask for twenty-five-hundred dollars a cartoon. However, the distributor had been working behind his back and had approached all of Disney's Oswald cartoonists. The deal would be eighteen-hundred dollars a cartoon or the staff would leave Disney's studio and create Oswald elsewhere.

Since Universal owned Oswald and Disney didn't, Walt found himself backed into a corner. He couldn't afford to make the cartoons at such a low price. On the other hand, Oswald was his major income-producer.

Disney was never one to give up. He decided to cut his losses and start again. The majority of the staff left, with the notable exception of Iwerks. Disney had learned that it was important to retain control of your creations.

Together, he and Ub began collaborating on a

new cartoon series about a mouse—a mouse they named Mortimer.

It was 1927 and the beginning of the "talkies." Disney was excited about the possibilities of adding sound to his animations. He went off to New York to gather information on how to put together a sound-track. He found that many companies were making records to accompany the films. But there seemed to be too many problems associated with this practice. Disney wanted a way to add sound to the film itself; otherwise everything might get out of sync.

He intuitively understood that now was the time to focus on sound. Talkies were going to be big business, and he wanted to be part of it. However, his first venture working with an orchestra and sound effects people was a disappointment. He'd invested over a thousand dollars to add sound to his mouse cartoon, and the music people didn't seem to understand how to pace the sound with the animations on the screen.

Disney decided to direct the next recording session himself. He told everyone what to do and when to do it, and he personally did the cartoon voices.

The results were what he'd hoped for. And he'd learned another valuable lesson: **Sometimes You Have To Do It Yourself.**

Now he just had to sell it. He showed his talking cartoon to several major distributors, but they were not enthusiastic. Disney couldn't understand it. He *knew* he had a winner.

A public relations man who was running a movie house on Broadway explained to Disney that the only way to sell the series was to create a public demand for it. To do that, he'd have to release it privately. The publicist, Harry Reichenbach, offered Disney five-hundred dollars a week for a two-week run of the first cartoon with sound, "Steamboat Willie," starring Mickey Mouse (Disney's wife had disliked the name Mortimer). Disney needed the money (as always) and accepted.

It was the right move at the right time.

Disney's creative triumph was heralded from *Variety* to *The New York Times*. Film distributors began calling. But Disney had learned his lesson with the Oswald fiasco. Mickey Mouse was his, and he wasn't selling the rights to anyone.

He eventually made an agreement for distribution with his sound company, Cinephone.

As the mouse took off, Disney kept creating and trying new ideas. He began working on animations to classical music and developed *The Skeleton Dance*, set to Grieg's "March of the Dwarfs." It didn't go over right away. With most new ideas, people initially reject the unfamiliar. But self-confident creators are persistent, and rejection does not get in their way. It was only a matter of time before Disney's "Silly Symphonies" were accepted, and between them and Mickey Mouse, he was becoming famous.

Not unlike Disney, who ventured to Hollywood, Milton Hershey decided it was time to establish himself in New York. With yet another loan from his Aunt Mattie, and the unfailing support of his mother, Milton went to work for a candy maker by day and cooked his own confections in his landlady's kitchen at night. It wasn't long before he had a following and enough money to open Hershey's Fine Candies on Sixth Avenue. Ever loyal, his mother and aunt came to help him. It was like old times in Philadelphia.

But the more successful he became, and the bigger his sales, the larger his debts grew. He constantly needed money for sugar, and his family kept loaning it to him. After three years of making a successful product that somehow kept losing money, Hershey had to close his doors again. By this time, he owed several thousand dollars, he was being evicted from both his apartment and his shop, and his equipment was about to be repossessed.

With his last dollars, Hershey managed to get some of his cookware to the railroad station, where he shipped it to himself in Pennsylvania collect and then bought a one-way ticket home. Since he had no money left, he ate what remained of his candy for dinner.

Hershey arrived back in his hometown (now Hershey, Pennsylvania) on a cold and rainy night. His mother's house was too far away to walk to, and he had no money. The next day his cooking equipment would arrive at the station, and he had no idea how he was going to pay for it. He wasn't even thirty years old and already he'd managed to fail at the same business in Philadelphia, Chicago, New Orleans and New York. By this time most people would have given up. But persistence is crucial.

For every door that closes, another one opens. Hershey had come home hoping to start again somehow. And as fate would have it, he ran into his old friend, Lebbie, from the Philadelphia days. Lebbie took Hershey in, fed him supper, ran him a hot bath, gave him dry clothes, and sent him to bed. Exhausted, Milton fell asleep. When he awoke the next morning, Lebbie had already retrieved the cookware, rented shop space, and was ready to invest his life savings to set up another candymaking business with Hershey. And it was this one that finally worked.

Now you may be saying that's all well and good for Hershey and Disney because even though they went bankrupt repeatedly, they always managed to find some money to get them started again. But what about me? I don't have an Aunt Mattie, or a Lebbie, or a brother Roy. My whole family thinks I'm nuts and they wouldn't loan me a nickel . . .

If that's the case, then you have to find other sources. You go to friends, you go to strangers. You swap, you barter, you trade. And you persist. Being at the right place at the right time helps, but first you have to *make it to* the right time. You have to *make it to* the right place. Timing is not just a matter of circumstance. It is a matter of persistence.

# IMAGINATION PLUS

$M$agic is an illusion, a thing of tricks and sleight of hand. It is making the impossible appear possible. It is perfect timing. We know rationally that those doves did not appear out of thin air, and yet it looks that way. Sometimes a magician is so good, we believe the illusion. We applaud the skill. We can't figure out how he did it and it doesn't matter. Behind every good magician is a lot of practice, a lot of planning and split-second timing. Behind every illusion is a solution, a step-by-step sequence.

Remember the old trick you did as a kid, when you snatched a coin from the palm of a friend's hand before he could close it? To make it work, you strike your friend's palm with your fingertips, which causes the coin to bounce in the air. You catch it as you're pulling your hand away. All precision timing!

Successful people work like magicians. Sometimes we only see the outcome—the illusion, if you will. We don't always see the steps that led to their success. We don't see how problems were worked through and solutions were obtained. But everything takes effort, planning, practice, common sense and timing.

The first step in solving problems starts with your imagination. Like common sense, we all have imagination, we just have to use it. Use your *common sense* to think of all the practical solutions to a problem. Use your *imagination* to think of all the improbable, wildcard solutions. Together, they can cover all possibilities.

Imagination is the flip side of common sense, and unless the two are working in tandem, you'll never get very far. You can have the most wonderful dreams in the world, but unless you use common sense, you will never implement one of them. You can be the most practical thinker there is, but if you can't dream for the future, you'll stay stuck in the same place, scared to take a risk. There's an old saying—the bigger the risk, the greater the reward . . .

## I WON'T DO IT!

Try this exercise. Make a list of all the things you would never do. Not things like going to the moon for NASA, but things that are possible, things your friends do. Perhaps you'd never fly in a helicopter, take the subway, eat sushi, go to a football game, go to the ballet, disagree with your boss, go to a movie alone, ride a horse, speak in public, wear a bikini. You name it, there is someone who won't do it.

Look over the list, and for everything you won't do, think about why you won't. The answer "because I don't like it" does not count unless you've recently tried it. Are you not trying these things because you're scared? Because you don't know how? Because you might look foolish? Why would you refuse to ride a horse? Lots of people ride horses, so obviously they are not as dangerous as great white sharks. They certainly can't eat you. If you don't know how to ride, that is easily remedied. There was a time when you didn't know how to drive. What about the risk of looking foolish? That's all in your head: inexperienced people look inexperienced, they don't look foolish. Everyone has a lot more respect for someone who is willing to try something new than for someone who whines "I can't." People who are willing to expand themselves will go further and be happier than those who never try to extend their reach. You are not perfect the way you are—no matter what your mother or your lover says.

Open your mind and imagine yourself riding that horse. What's the worst that could happen? You could fall off and be seriously injured, maybe even maimed or killed. But so what? As bad or worse can happen to you any time you ride in a car or train or airplane, but that doesn't mean you walk everywhere you want to go. You have to put these things in perspective. You're not busting broncos in a Wild West show, right? So stop worrying and ride the horse. Believe me, the horse is trained, even if you're not. So, for your own personal growth, go ride that horrible horse!

## LEARN TO SAY, "WHY NOT?"

Sometimes trying one new thing opens a whole world of new perspectives for you. The world looks different when you're on horseback! You couldn't really imagine it even if you tried. You have to say "YES!" You have to say, "Why not?" You not only must learn to take advantage of opportunities, but to create them.

Accept your inexperience in some areas and set out to change yourself. More often than not, you'll enjoy yourself. You'll prove you're capable of doing challenging things. You're not as scared or inadequate as you anticipated. And it's always easier the next time.

What you're doing is building self-confidence and stretching your imagination. Everything you attempt adds to your progress in life. You have a fifty-fifty chance in succeeding in whatever you try. And you can easily make those odds more in your favor.

I once interviewed a professional blackjack dealer. He taught me that there are only so many times you can lose. If you play one hundred hands of blackjack, you have a fifty-fifty chance of winning each hand. You could lose the first fifty hands (unlikely), but you will never lose all one hundred hands. Professional players keep betting even when they seem to be on a losing streak, because the odds are that it will change.

Professional players also work with statistics. They count cards to change the odds in their favor. If you can up the chances of winning from fifty-fifty to seventy-thirty by paying attention to what is going on around you, that is using both common sense and timing. You want the odds in your favor no matter what you're doing.

## A NEW LINE OF CREDIT

When I started my magazine, the odds against my succeeding were about two thousand to one. That's because there is a very high failure rate for new magazines, and I had very little capital. I had only forty-five hundred dollars, and I needed about two and a half million dollars to make the magazine work.

I knew I had a great idea. I knew I could make it work. It was just a matter of using common sense to make the forty-five hundred work as effectively as the two and a half million. I now have a multimillion-dollar publishing empire, all built through common sense and timing—but when I first started, I didn't have enough money to go out and rent an office.

My first office was in the unheated basement of a funeral home. The rent was fifty dollars a month. The man rented me a room because he felt sorry for me. As a matter of fact, he gave me the room where they used to embalm the bodies. I made my office as nice as possible on the limited funds I had. Paint is cheap and makes even a basement look bright and cheerful.

I installed a phone and I was ready for business. But the world wasn't beating a path to my door. I got one or two letters a week addressed to *Resident* or *Occupant*. The phone rang twice a day—one wrong number and one call from my wife wondering when I was coming home for dinner!

Meanwhile, I was spending money like crazy putting ads in the newspaper for salespeople. I knew that one of the most important resources of any magazine is the salespeople. They bring in the advertising revenue needed to pay the bills.

Soon I had run up a large advertising bill with the local newspapers, and I found myself unable to get credit for more ads. How was I going to keep paying for advertising? I needed to place at least two thousand dollars worth of advertising within the next two months, so I could assure myself a constant flow of applicants until I found the right people to work for me.

Since the newspapers wouldn't give me any more credit, I had to use my common sense. In thinking about the possibilities available to me (not many), I realized that the newspapers were billing me according to my telephone number. My billing account number was the same as my phone number! After I realized that, it made sense to install a new phone line with a new phone number which automatically gave me a new line of credit from which I could keep advertising. I couldn't charge any more advertising on my old phone number since I had an outstanding balance of three thousand dollars. It was so easy to pay thirty dollars for a new phone line and start with a new line of credit!

Now I know some people wouldn't have done this. Some people wouldn't have taken a room at the undertakers, either. They would have taken their forty-five hundred dollars and invested it in something safe.

But if you can't take a risk, how can you gain anything? **You've got to believe in your own ability to succeed!** Sometimes you take two steps backwards to go four steps forward. Sometimes you have to go into debt.

I've cited Hershey and Disney because they are great examples of American entrepreneurship. They started poor. They worked hard. They made money. They lost money. They struggled. They lost more money. They went into debt, even into bankruptcy. But they kept moving forward. Persevering. Trying.

Disney was amazingly imaginative. He was always perfecting what was already done while working on something entirely new. Even though Mickey Mouse was making him famous, he had other ideas he wanted to try. Since he didn't have the financial independence to do exactly as he wanted (yet), he signed a new contract with Columbia Pictures at seven-thousand dollars per cartoon. But Disney kept hiring better artists to do more complicated cartooning. Not unlike Hershey, Disney had an enor-mouse-ly successful product and a precarious financial position. In the early years of the Depression, he often couldn't meet his payroll. He tried to negotiate with Columbia, asking them for fifteen-thousand dollars per cartoon, but they thought he was crazy. When the contract expired, Disney went elsewhere.

Charlie Chaplin was a great fan of Disney's work. He thought Disney was a genius, and so he pushed for his studio, United Artists, to sign this master of animation. UA agreed, and at the price Disney wanted.

It was at this point in time that a company called Technicolor introduced a way to add color to films. This appealed to Disney's imagination. He knew his company had to have it! His brother argued that they couldn't afford color cartoons, but Walt was sure it would pay off in the long run. He made a two-year deal with Technicolor and then personally worked with the lab technicians to perfect the color process for his cartoons.

His instincts were correct. The first color "Silly Symphony" was a resounding success. Disney's studio began attracting top-notch creative artists, and Disney established his own animation school at the studio to train them.

In 1933, Disney made *The Three Little Pigs* complete with sound, color, and its own theme song ("Who's Afraid of the Big Bad Wolf?"). It was a phenomenal success. The whole country began singing the song, and Disney's studio began collecting music royalties. A new business of scoring and songwriting became part of the cartoon enterprise (see how one thing often unexpectedly leads to another?).

By this time, Disney employed more than a hundred eighty people, and he wanted to make a feature-length animated film. He decided on *Snow White*. The proposed five-hundred-thousand-dollar budget boggled his advisers' minds, but Disney was sure of himself. The idea of an eighty-minute cartoon with animated humans thoroughly challenged him. He knew what he wanted to do and how it should look, and he went about inventing ways to achieve that vision. By the time the project was completed, *Snow White* was triple the projected costs, and rumor had dubbed the cartoon "Disney's Folly." It was released for Christmas in 1937. Its overwhelming success is history.

When Hershey began his candy business again in his hometown (remember, this was his fifth venture), he had learned an important lesson: no matter how in demand your product is, you can't make money selling it only in the neighborhood. Using his experience and imagination, Hershey invented a new kind of caramel made with milk, which he named "Crystal A's." Not only did they become popular with the penny-candy crowd, but orders began coming in from wholesalers. As the demand increased, Hershey hired more people to work for him. It was no longer just a family operation. He finally realized he didn't have to do everything himself. If he hired good help, he'd be free to experiment, to create new confections, and to socialize with other business and tradespeople. Nowadays we call it networking.

Through his local banker, Hershey met an English importer who began ordering large quantities of Crystal A's. The familiar cycle of high demand and higher debt began to plague Hershey again. Another infusion of cash came when his aunt volunteered her house as collateral for a bank loan. When the loan came due, Hershey didn't have the capital to pay it. Discouraged, he went to discuss the situation with his banker, and was amazed to find a check for two thousand five hundred dollars from his importer waiting for his endorsement. The exchange rates were working in Hershey's favor!

The next time Hershey needed money for expansion, his banker suggested they go to New York for the necessary funding. This time he had no problem getting credit. His caramels and his purchase orders spoke for themselves.

The bank gave Hershey a two-hundred fifty thousand dollar building loan to expand. Business snowballed, Hershey hired more managers and expanded his original factory until it took up almost the whole block, with 450,000 square feet of floor space.

His chief caramel competitor was in Chicago, so he decided to build a new factory there. In a short time Hershey owned four factories and was making more money than he could count. The demands from his English importer were still increasing. Hershey was intrigued. What were they doing with all that caramel? He decided to take a trip to London. His curiosity changed his life—and America's. The British were dipping the caramel in chocolate before packing it!

Hershey recognized the potential for chocolate-covered candy. He came home, expanded his herd of milk cows, and ordered a German chocolate-rolling machine. The rest is history. He went on to experiment with all sorts of milk and chocolate combinations. He trusted his taste buds and perfected his creations down to the last detail (including putting his name on every single Hershey's Kiss). He hired his help by instinct and eventually built a whole town for his workers centered around his original family homestead. He established a school for orphaned boys, married for love, worked hard, and died with much loyalty, affection, respect, money and success.

Sounds easy, doesn't it? It should only happen to all of us. But have you noticed the common thread through all these success stories? Hard work, yes. Persistence, yes. And money. Money, money, money! Because money makes money. Sometimes it takes a while to get into position—look at how many times Hershey tried. But you have to be willing to take the risks, to play with money.

## THE LAST TABOO

People have a lot of hang-ups about money. We'll discuss the most intimate details of our sex lives, but money is still taboo. We like having it; we don't like borrowing it; and we can't get enough of it. We don't like owing it and we don't like paying it back.

Get more comfortable with money. It's just a tool. It's a barter system. We don't want to be working for it, we want it working for us.

You might say your goal is to have a lot of money, but just imagine what that means. Visualize it. I'm sure you don't picture yourself sitting in a room surrounded by millions of dollars. What you picture are the things that money can be traded for.

Most successful people are not working for the money itself. They're working for the rewards, for the satisfaction. They're working to win! They're working for the challenge of it.

It's like playing cards for toothpicks. If the goal is toothpicks, you see how many toothpicks you can win. The only person who can measure how successful you are is *you*. If you measure that success in dollars, then by all means try to amass as many as you can.

I think you'll find along the way that your standards of measurement will change. When you were little, you were busy accumulating baseball cards or Barbie clothes. You compared how many you had to how many your friends had. As you got a little older, you stopped counting the number and started focusing on the quality. Now it didn't matter if you had fifty baseball cards, or a hundred Barbie outfits, as long as you had the *right* baseball cards, the *right* outfits. So it goes. Eventually you will outgrow your focus on quantity and begin thinking about quality. You'll realize it's not how much you have, it's what you have— it's *WHO YOU ARE*. It's how you think.

## SURVIVAL TEST

There was an interesting survival test that Green Beret candidates had to pass. It was essentially a common sense test to see if the soldiers could analyze problems and handle them wisely.

In the test, you are dropped off on an island. On that island is a Jeep. On the seat is a note saying that the Jeep is out of gas. You have to get the Jeep across a bridge, on the other side of which is a fifty-gallon gas drum. However, you can only go over the bridge once.

Next to the Jeep is an open-top tube eight inches in diameter and four feet high. It is half-filled with gasoline, but cemented into the ground so it can't be removed.

One foot from the top of the tube there is a hole with a hose coming out of it. The problem is (seemingly) obvious. How do you get the gasoline out of the tube and into the Jeep so you can go over the bridge? You have to do something to cause the gasoline to rise in the tube as high as the hose. You could drop rocks down the tube and cause the gasoline level to rise. Or you could . . .

But wait. Reevaluate the situation. The common sense solution is right in front of you all the time. Hit the starter. The note is a lie. The Jeep had a full tank of gas all the time.

Many soldiers spent a great deal of time problem-solving because they assumed that there was no gas. DO NOT ASSUME! Check to make sure a problem really exists before you waste time and energy trying to solve it!

Several years ago, two young men had to deliver a truck of ice cream. It was summer. It was hot. And on the way to their destination, the truck broke down. They knew it was just a matter of time before the

95-degree heat started doing its job, and with the image of melting ice cream, they also saw their profit melting away.

As luck would have it, they had broken down on a main road. One of the young men decided they might as well try to sell the ice cream while it was still hard, and he fashioned a sign advertising ice cream at five cents a scoop. This was a novel idea and people began to stop and take advantage of this roadside treat.

This young, imaginative entrepreneur was not about to lose money. His name was Tom Carvel. He used his common sense and passed his own survival test.

Remember the old shell game? Someone puts a dried pea under one of three shells and then moves the shells around. You have to guess which one has the pea under it. If you've played it, chances are you've never guessed right. After the shells have been shuffled around you've pointed to the one you're sure has the pea under it. The person doing the trick picks up the shell, and invariably there's nothing under it. Therefore you lose. How could you win? Is the hand really quicker than the eye?

The answer is: yes. There's a trick to the game. The person moving the shell deftly removes the pea when he lifts the shell you've picked. The solution, using your common sense, is to pick up the correct shell yourself. That way he can't make the pea disappear. But what if he removed the pea even before he started moving the shells? There's an answer there, too. When you have to choose, pick up both of the empty shells at once. That leaves one shell that *has* to have the pea under it—and if the pea isn't there, that's the trickster's problem.

When you have a problem to solve, remember that there is always more than one solution. Keep this in mind and stack the odds in your favor.

## THINKING SMALL
## AND THINKING BIG

I remember when two of my friends started landscaping companies. Neither of them had much money to get started, but there the similarity ended.

Bob went out and bought only the basics he felt were necessary to start. He figured he would add a piece of equipment each month and grow from there as money started coming in. But Bob couldn't take on any big jobs because he didn't have the necessary tools yet. He established a good neighborhood business, but there were no big accounts. Because of his cash-flow problem, he spent a lot of time scouting for bargains. The cheap equipment he bought often broke down, and there were a lot of repair expenses, costly in both time and money (remember, time is money).

Joe, on the other hand, used his common sense. He planned what equipment he would need, and drew up a budget of estimated costs. He concluded he needed about forty-three thousand dollars to start a complete working business and keep it afloat for a year. Joe didn't have forty-three thousand dollars, so he borrowed it. Then he bought everything he needed.

Joe spent most of his time making money doing the big jobs Bob couldn't take on. In four months, Joe made enough money to pay back his loan.

Nine months later, Bob went out of business. Joe took over all his equipment and accounts and hired Bob as one of his supervisors!

Bob thought small and Joe thought big. Big ideas and big dreams helped Joe become successful. He believed in himself and was willing to take a few risks. Common sense told Joe he had to be properly financed to succeed. The main reason most businesses fail is the lack of money. You have to *have* money to make money. And if you don't have any, use your common sense to get some!

Let me tell you a little story about common sense. There was a time when I was down and out and everything was going wrong. I wasn't making any money. I was three months behind in all my bills and over three hundred thousand dollars in debt. My wife, who was working, had just told me the good news— we were expecting our first baby! The very next day the bank handed me a foreclosure notice on my investment house—the only thing making any money for me at the time.

I had bought the house when I was just out of college. My parents were only charging me thirty-five dollars a week for room and board, but I wanted my privacy. I found out I could buy my own house and pay only one-hundred fifty dollars a month in mortgage payments! When I got married, I moved into another house and rented out my first one. A good thing, too, because just a few years later I was using all my rental income to finance my business (instead of to pay the mortgage and taxes).

I really believed that I was just in the building period and that it was only a matter of time before my business took off. Meanwhile, I was sweating it out. My borrowing power was all used up. I borrowed from my friends, the bank, my credit cards, my parents. There was no one left to borrow from, and my only source of steady income was about to be foreclosed.

I had to rely on common sense. I had no other choice but to fight the bank in court.

The bank wanted twenty-one thousand dollars to pay off the final balance, but they might as well have been asking for a million dollars. I was broke. Since I had the mortgage with the bank, I knew they were responsible for paying the taxes. I hired an attorney for a thousand dollars, arranging five payments of two-hundred dollars each. My plan was to tie up the bank as long as possible, so I could get on my feet. And it worked. While the foreclosure was being contested, I was still collecting my rent, and I was not responsible for making any mortgage or tax payments!

After two years, the case came to court. The bank wanted to work out a settlement, but I was just beginning to get my business off the ground and still couldn't afford to pay for the house or the back taxes. I turned down the deal the bank offered me because I still needed more time. When the case came up in court, I lost and was required to pay the bank all the back taxes, plus attorneys' fees, plus the principal and interest.

I had to stall for more time. Using common sense, I appealed the case because I knew how badly the courts were jammed. That gave me another fourteen months. When the case was about to come up again, I was in a much better position creditwise than before, although there was still a cash-flow problem. Since the mortgage on the house I was living in was finally up-to-date, I applied for a home equity loan on it.

The loan came through before the case came up. I put the money in the bank so I wouldn't spend it and started collecting interest on forty-one thousand dollars. When the case finally was called, I didn't even show up in court because I was prepared to lose. But I had the money to pay. When I lost in court, I had another thirty days to come up with the money before the actual foreclosure would take place.

I owed the bank a total of forty-one thousand dollars, including the twenty-one thousand dollars mortgage balance, taxes, and attorneys' fees for four years! What a deal! In four years I had collected rent. I paid the bank the balance with the money I had from my home equity loan; I made a profit of interest from the forty-one thousand dollars in the bank. I took a tax deduction on four years of back taxes and interest payments, and though I lost in court, I had won! I won by using common sense and timing!

## A FISH STORY

When people say, "Where there's a will, there's a way," what they're reminding us is that very little of what we want is simply given to us. We have to work for what we want, not only at our jobs, but using the tools we're born with: our common sense and the knowledge of when to strike—timing.

I was on vacation in the Bahamas as a guest of the Prime Minister and the Bahamian Tourism Bureau. As I went outside my villa (Howard Hughes' old escape place), I came across my eight-year old son, Mikey, looking wistfully at a 135-foot, sixteen-million-dollar yacht.

I said, "Mikey, how do you like that big boat?" Mikey replied that he loved it and wanted to know if I would buy him one when he got older. I told him "No," and Mikey looked at me with a sad, rejected face.

"Why, Daddy?" he asked.

"Mikey, I have a better idea," I told him. "I will show you how to make money, so you can buy it yourself."

Mikey replied: "Dad, that's a great idea, because when you show me how to make money I will buy you one, too!"

Then, as I stood looking into the crystal-clear water, my other two sons, Mark and Brian, came up to me. They asked me what I was looking at. I pointed down at the schools of fish swimming by. Their eyes lit up; they were enchanted. The next question—and I had a feeling this was coming—was: "Daddy, can you buy us some fish?"

I looked into their little brown eyes with their smiles from ear to ear, and told them I had a better idea. I went into the fishing shed and brought back three fishing poles with bait. I then gave them a lesson on how to catch a fish, and knowledge to show them they are capable of doing it by themselves. They caught a fish each, and we all had a great time.

The next day when I got up, I looked out the window and saw all three boys fishing. Each had caught a fish with no help from Dad. Independence had arrived.

## THE
## STRESS MESS

Whether things go bad,
they all seem to go bad at the same time. Bad luck
comes in batches—you can count on it! You get
overloaded at work, your car breaks down, your rent
check bounces, there's no time for yourself. Everything
that was going along so smoothly is attacked by
gremlins! You shake your head and wonder what's
going to happen next. How can you possibly deal with
it? You are juggling too many things and there is not
enough time.

When you find yourself in this discouraging situation, you feel under more pressure to get everything
done. Decisions have to be made. There is no time to
wait. And yet, this is probably the very worst time to
decide to do anything! You're overloaded. Your timing

has got to be off. When you're not in control of things, you'll make hasty or forced decisions that could very well lead to disaster.

You know when you're not yourself, when you're out of sorts. *Don't* keep going. Realize you are not going to accomplish anything major when you're feeling down, and get out of the situation. Take a break. Take a walk. Have a milkshake and a cheeseburger. Call an old friend. Go to the movies. You have to slow down, take it easy, rest. Do a few things to pamper yourself.

I know, it won't fix the problems or pay the bills. But the point is to give yourself a little TLC (tender loving care), catch your breath, get a second wind, a fresh perspective.

Stress plays a unique role in everyone's life. You can try and keep away from it, but like a cat stalking a bird, it sometimes creeps up from behind and pounces! People have different limits of tolerance. Some people can handle any mishaps on the home front as long as they're in control at work. Others let business problems roll off their back, but can't deal with stress at home. We've all seen people who function under the most stressful situations with grace and humor, and we marvel at how they manage it.

Their secret is simple—they know it could be worse!

# BURN-OUT

Stress comes from worrying. Often you're trying to do too many things at once and you don't know how you're going to manage it all. One more unanticipated situation upsets the applecart. You feel as though you just can't keep going. Everything's wearing you out. Psychologists call it burn-out.

Visualize a rocket going up. When all that rocket fuel is consumed, the rocket booster detaches and nosedives into the sea. When you come to the limits of your energy, you go into a nosedive, too. Burn-out is when your body and mind, your physical condition and ambition, all give out at once.

You don't have any energy. You know you have to get things done, but you can't get organized. You get lazy. You get bored. You become a poor sleeper. Either you sleep for hours, escaping the stress, or you sleep fitfully. Either way, you don't feel rested. You lose interest in sex. You become irritable, you get angry faster. You can't control your temper. If you're a smoker, you smoke more. If you're a coffee drinker, you drink more. You become emotionally sensitive, thin-skinned. Innocent remarks seem aimed at you personally. Because you're under growing pressure and strain, you have frequent headaches, backaches, stomach aches, skin irritations.

Your diet changes. Your body might crave fats or salt or sugar. Your appetite increases dramatically as you seek solace in food. You gain weight and get depressed about looking fat. Or you lose interest in food, lose weight and look like hell. Either way, you don't feel good and you don't like the way you look.

## PUT ON THE BRAKES

When you slip into this kind of slump (and everyone does occasionally), you have to get yourself out. Your timing is off. You have to rely on your common sense. You have to change the odds to work with you instead of against you. Stem the negativity and put yourself into a positive state of mind. How do you do that? Things have deteriorated so much, how can you possibly get back in control?

STOP! Stop whatever you're doing. Put the brakes on and reevaluate. You have to construct a new game plan and reorganize yourself. The most important advice is to STOP! RELAX! Take a break. Take a short vacation.

Don't say you can't. Don't rationalize that you have too much to do and that a break will make you fall further behind. You need to remove yourself from all the stress. Visualize the entire negative mess you've gotten enmeshed in. See it as a tangible thing you can separate yourself from. *You* are not the mess. You are just surrounded by it—rather like Indiana Jones when he fell into the pit of snakes. You have to step out of the situation and try to get some perspective. Leave the bad times—the snakes—where they are and go somewhere else. Stop thinking about them. They'll stay exactly where they are, waiting for you to come back. I'm not advocating that you flee to South America and never return. Just take a little R & R.

## TROUBLE IN BLACK AND WHITE

It's important to decide how to tackle your problems, but before you can do that, you have to stop abusing yourself. When you burn out, you start to feel sorry for yourself. You don't take care of yourself. You feel stupid or incompetent. You feel ugly and clumsy. Nothing is important and you don't care anyway; so there! But you know deep down that you're just goofing off. Nobody's going to come and rescue you. You have to rescue yourself!

Start moving out of your depression with simple common sense actions. Take a shower. Fix your hair. Put on an outfit you know you look good in (even if you don't think you look good right now). Go out for breakfast. Pretend you are a perfectly normal person whose world is not falling apart. Have the orange juice, the bacon, the works.

Now make a list of all the awful things in your life. Put them in writing. If you can put them in writing, you can limit them. They are defined. They are in black and white. You have now taken the first step for success.

## PRIORITIZE

Maybe you are trying to juggle six disasters at once. You're getting laid off from your job, your landlord's selling your house, the muffler fell off your car, you can't pay your MasterCard, and your best friend is very ill. What can you do? What do you do first? (Besides crawling into your bed and pulling the covers over your head.)

First you have to get your priorities straight: decide which of these calamities you can do something about, and which you can only react to. You can get the easy ones out of the way first or you can tackle the hardest one first.

Of these five, the car problem is the simplest. You need a new muffler. The MasterCard bill is another easy one. You either pay or you don't. The solution is not an emotional one. It's black and white (or in this case, green or not-green).

Sometimes you have to start with what is stressing you most emotionally. Is it having to find a new job or a new apartment? Is it your friend's illness?

Some stress you have no control over. You can't do a thing to change your friend's prognosis, but you can change how you're dealing with it. Are you feeling sorry for yourself or for your friend? So go visit him. If he lives in California and you're broke in New York, call him up. Why wait to send flowers? Borrow the money for an airline ticket. Stop being inert! Deal with the situation NOW! This is one problem situation you don't have time to mope about. Remember—you may not have another chance.

What about the rest of your hassles? It looks like you need a new job and a new place to live. What's so bad about that? Perhaps you're just afraid to get out of your comfortable rut and make some changes in your life. You feel you have lost control of the decision-making process. But that's not true; you have lots of choices to make. While it was not your decision to leave either your job or apartment, what comes next is totally up to you. You must make a plan according to the time frame you're left with. When will your current job be ending? Can you collect unemployment? Will they give you references? Does your boss have any suggestions? Are other people leaving too? Talk to them. What are their plans? Read the papers. Start tracking down leads. Do you really want to stay in the same field? Now might be just the time to try something new. What have you been dreaming about? Can you go for it? You have nothing to lose and everything to gain!

The same thing is true for your housing situation. When do you have to be out? Did your landlord sell the house yet or is he just considering it? Can you buy it?

Stop looking at all these situations as disasters. Try considering them as opportunities. Take the attitude that things happen for the best. A job change could mean more money, more contracts, more satisfaction. Focus on them as beginnings, not the endings. You're capable of taking control of your life and making some exciting choices. There are a lot of possibilities!

## KEEP GOING

Sometimes you just feel out of sorts. There's nothing awful in your life. Your job is satisfying, your spouse is sweet, your bills are paid. Everything is running smoothly. It's just that you feel disjointed. Something's missing. But since you seem to have everything, what could be wrong? Take a look at your goals. Where are you going? What do you want to accomplish? Sometimes we reach a point where we've achieved the goals and have nothing new to look forward to. We seem successful, but we're stagnating. Where did the challenge go? How can we get it back?

This time the key is to keep going. You should have both short-range goals and ultimate long-range goals. If you're stuck in a monetarily fruitful but mentally fruitless situation, look for something else to do. It's time for a change. You do not need your standard vacation to get your dissatisfaction under control; you need a totally new perspective to dissolve your ennui.

Volunteer some of your time. Read to the blind. Deliver lunch one day a week for Meals on Wheels. Volunteer at the local church soup kitchen. Answer phones at a hotline crisis center. Call your local social services and give something of yourself. You need a jolt of realism in your complacent life, one that will put the gusto back into your work life, or give you the boost you need to change direction.

## MAKE LIFE EASIER

Often our stress is coming from outside us—work pressures, social pressures, too much to do and not enough time. We have to get back to the basic idea of focusing.

Exactly where is all the stress coming from? Think about what can be eliminated. Sometimes we give everything a ten-star priority when it doesn't deserve so much attention. Don't try to solve more than one problem at a time. Sometimes executives get tied down at work because they are doing ten jobs at once. They start to get confused. Stress sets in, and interruption after interruption takes place, and nothing gets accomplished.

Finish one job at a time and make sure you delegate some of the work. Share your responsibility. Make the person you assign work to feel important about that assignment.

You are responsible for your own success. You are also responsible for making your life easier.

## BREAKING PATTERNS

If you had six months to live, what would you be doing? What would matter? Give yourself some time. Schedule what you *want* to do as well as what you *have* to do. Rethink what you have to do. What would happen if you didn't do it?

Sometimes we get so busy agreeing to do everything and go everywhere that our lives are not particularly pleasurable, nor are they our own.

People get stuck in the programs of their past.

They do things a certain way because that's how their parents did them, because that's how they were taught. There's no discrimination involved, no right and wrong. There's only the sameness, the static marching in place.

There are always more ways than one to do anything. You have to incorporate that flexibility in your everyday thinking. You don't necessarily have to change your ways; just be open to the fact that other ways exist and they might even be quicker, better, nicer. Or even just different!

It is up to you to change your patterns, since you set up the patterns to begin with. You have to learn when to stop, when to start over.

I once did a study of a hundred successful people. At some time in every one of their lives, they had undergone these feelings of despair and depression. Every one of them. One hundred percent.

You are not alone.

How did they get out of their ruts? Each person had different methods, but the bottom line was common sense and timing. Each was at a low point in his life, so when an opportunity came up (timing), he had nothing to lose; he went for it (common sense).

## THE END RUN

Opportunities do come up, but you must look for them. Make the effort and try to find them. Don't wait for something to happen. Go out and make it happen!

Let me give you an example of something that happened to me. My job was to sell advertising space. The usual method is to zero in on the prospective client, then find out their advertising agency. From there, you track down the agency's account executive handling that particular client, then the media planner and the media buyer. These people are in charge of millions of advertising dollars. They can make or break you. After you give them a presentation, they have to call a meeting to discuss whether or not your service is good for their client. This sometimes takes up to six months or a year!

This is all wasted time for someone like me trying to sell advertising space. In my opinion, most of these executive decision-makers probably couldn't sell their product to wholesalers or consumers if their lives depended on it! If the tables were turned, they wouldn't survive. It's ironic how people in marketing make decisions on how to sell a product they couldn't sell themselves. Sometimes you reach a numbers person whose only interest is how many people you can reach for every dollar spent (better known as cost per thousands). Take away that person's calculator and they are lost

All this is very frustrating to a salesperson. Not all advertising agencies are this bad, but they all have a chain of command you must follow to get the advertising or insertion order.

After going two full years without any insertion orders from some of the companies I'd been pursuing, I got smart and used some common sense. I went directly to the client—the person who has the final decision, the person who says yes or no. The client doesn't report to the advertising agency; the advertising agency reports to the client. So I broke the rule; I went around the advertising agency.

Common sense told me I'd had no business from them—a big fat minus so far—so I had nothing to lose by going to the client directly. If the client gave me a zero, it was still a plus . . . because now I was sure they had been told about the product.

Guess what happened? That's right! The first time I made my presentation, I came back with my first national client! The decision was made on the spot. The client was J&B Scotch. For two years I'd been trying to sell the agencies, and the answer to my problem was to go around them! I found out that the agency does whatever the client wants. What usually takes six months or a year only took me one hour.

I still had to deal with the agency, but it's a lot different with the insertion order in your hand.

With this example in mind, always remember that there are several ways to solve and handle each problem. The more experience you have recognizing problems, the easier it will be to recognize solutions and techniques to solve them.

## THE SUCCESS SCALE

In your life you will be faced with thousands of decisions that will relate to your success. Before you make any choices, break down the issue into a minus (-), a zero (0), or a plus (+)— my Success Scale.

Think of it as a thermometer. All you want it to do

is go up. If you are working with a minus with nothing to lose, why not make the effort? The worst that will happen is that you will reach a dead end, a zero. If you're at a zero, use your imagination. There has to be a way (or two or three) around that blockade. And if you're already in a plus situation, just keep going!

Everyone has a different platform of success. Ask anyone if they'd like to make a lot of money. Almost everyone will say yes. But they'll mean different things. For some it will mean fifty thousand dollars a year; for others, one-hundred thousand dollars; for others, much more. Your standards of living, financial needs and material values determine your platform of success.

When you're out of sorts, think about how much worse it could be. You could be careless, jobless, useless. You could be disabled, handicapped, terminally ill. None of your catastrophes amount to a hill of beans in the long-range scheme of things. If you want to wallow in a little self-pity for a while, that's your prerogative—but try to keep it short and get on with the things at hand. You can always exercise some sort of control.

You are responsible for your own actions and reactions. You can change *you*, even if you can't change anything or anyone else. And that is the essence of common sense and timing—the evolutionary change of you—your growth, your experience, your control over your life's progress. Go for it!

## GO FOR IT!

*"The first million is the hardest."*

—Milton Hershey

## EVERY EFFORT POSSIBLE AND EVERY POSSIBLE EFFORT

Everyone has an equal shot at being successful. If you don't start somewhere, you won't get anywhere!

One of the biggest problems people have today is that they make their problems bigger than they are. That saying about making a mountain out of a molehill applies to all of us. The bigger the problem becomes in your mind, the harder it is to solve! The harder problems seem, the more stress they cause. Let's face it—no problem is worse than death. So anything else is just what we make it. We might as well make it work! We might as well go for it.

If you have a goal you really want to reach, you must be determined that no one is going to stop you. (I assume this is a legal goal.) Your determination will help you keep the will power to make every effort possible and to make every possible effort. In my survey of over two thousand people, eighty-three percent responded that they do not always make a full effort or apply themselves a hundred percent towards their goals. Why not?

If something is important to you, why don't you put forth your best effort? Why do you let other things interfere? What are you afraid of? You've already learned how to focus your energies and attention and how to solve problems. Perhaps we should look at the down side of success. What happens if you do succeed? What is the worst thing that would happen if you put forth your best effort and went the whole nine yards? What might happen to you if you started making five hundred thousand dollars a year? Are you afraid you'd spend it all foolishly? Are you worried your pals might hit you up for loans and you wouldn't be able to refuse?

Don't laugh. Many of us harbor a secret fear of success.

Perhaps if you had the money, you'd take action on that divorce; maybe you'd have time to write that book; maybe you'd design that beach hideaway or take flying lessons or whatever it is you say you'd do *if only* you had the opportunity. Sometimes having the opportunity is scary, and the possibility of success brings with it many hidden fears. Do you really want to live out all the daydreams you've ever had? Perhaps you don't put forth your best effort because winning would eliminate your fantasies. What will be left for you if you succeed?

# STEPPING STONES

Don't forget that life is a series of stepping stones. Sometimes we go forward, sometimes back—sometimes we just sidestep. But we never get blocked in *all* directions. The problem is often that we're comfortable where we are, even if it's not where we really want to be. We're in a nice little niche and change would bring the unknown. If we knew what would happen, we wouldn't hesitate. But we're all a little afraid to find out. We can get psyched up for failure well enough, but we don't get psyched up for success. If we did, we'd be a lot further ahead.

Did any of you men ever want to be a professional football or baseball player? Did any of you women dream about being a model or actress? Did any of you ever try going for it?

Did you know that anyone can get an application to try out for any pro team? Just call the team of your choice and they will tell you when tryouts are. This doesn't mean you are going to make the team, but at least you will have tried! Just because a person is in professional sports doesn't necessarily mean they are the best. It really means that out of all the people who've tried out and made the effort, these players are the best. There are lots of great athletes who never make the effort to turn pro. It's not their priority. There are probably some terrific natural athletes who have no interest in playing a particular sport. It's not important to them.

When the National Football League went on strike, the owners had replacement teams in one day! Six days later these guys were on the field as professional football players. They were the "pros." One week these men were selling cars, building houses, teaching kids, mowing lawns, bartending—and the next week they were on TV playing professional football with millions of people watching them! The funny thing about it was that some of those guys were better than the striking players who retained jobs in the NFL. All of this was possible for these guys because they used their common sense and timing and made the effort to get involved in pro football.

Lots of women think they have to be beautiful to become an actress or model. Wrong! Sometimes it helps, but it's not necessary. The movie and television industries use all kinds of people. Pick up a copy of *Show Business* magazine. Each issue has casting news. There is a demand for all body sizes—small, medium, large, extra-large. There is work for the handicapped. There are lots of opportunities available. It's just a matter of going for it! And that's all up to you.

In the survey I mentioned before, I asked the

question: Would you like to become a famous movie star? Ninety-seven percent said yes. The follow-up question was: Did you ever apply for a position in the movie or modeling industry? Ninety-five percent said no. Common sense tells you that your chances for getting an acting or modeling job are nil if you haven't even applied for one.

If you are the only person who knows you want a certain kind of job, what good is it doing you? That's why networking has become so important today. Networking is the process of exposing who you are and what you do to people in related fields. Talk to everyone you can about what you do and what you *want* to do. Pass around your business cards and exchange phone numbers. (If you don't have any business cards, get some made. They're a modern necessity). Networking is a major part of getting where you want to go. It's one of those stepping stones that could lead in any direction.

Don't ever say you can't! Eliminate the word "can't" from your vocabulary. You can say it might be difficult. You can even admit it will be hard. But don't say you *can't* unless you have given it more than your best shot and approached it from every angle. Remember—somebody can. And it might as well be you!

Self-motivation and effort will conquer almost anything. Tenacity also helps. Be sure to give yourself a little reward just for trying. Make a deal with yourself —if you try to do X, you will give yourself Z. Everyone likes a pat on the back or a little reward or praise. Sometimes you have to give it to yourself. Sometimes no one else really knows what you're doing or trying to achieve. Eventually your efforts will start being noticed, but in the meantime be your own cheering section. And don't let setbacks stand in your way. Use them to solidify your determination.

Remember when Disney went out on a limb to make *Snow White,* and everyone expected it to flop and it didn't? It was a wonderful success. But he didn't go on from there to make only hit after hit. No one does.

After *Snow White,* the Disney brothers were a bit dizzy with their achievement, and they expanded again, building a three million dollar studio. Disney then made *Pinocchio, Fantasia* and *Bambi.* They were all critically acclaimed, but none of them made the kind of money *Snow White* made. By 1940, Disney was in debt again—this time for four and a half million dollars! The studio decided to go public and sold stock.

This infusion of cash helped, but then Disney ran into problems with the newly-organized unions. Then there were the war years. The army took over a large part of the studio, and Disney was engaged in making training films and a propaganda film called *Victory Through Air Power.* After World War II, the Disney brothers found themselves still over four million dollars in debt and with nothing new on the drawing board.

Disney wanted to do another feature film—he had *Peter Pan* in mind—but the financial pressure was on to produce shorter, quicker, money-making films. The studio put out a number of short cartoons based on popular music, including the classic *Peter and the Wolf.* And Disney began working on a live action film with cartoon figures—*Song of the South.* Its release in 1946 was welcomed, but it wasn't a money-maker.

With Disney Studios deep in debt, the company began taking orders to do educational films and instructional cartoons for big corporations. They were shifting into advertising, and Walt wasn't at all satisfied. This wasn't what he wanted to do. This wasn't what he was all about. This wasn't entertainment.

No one works well on scared money. You can't focus on what you're capable of doing when you're looking at the world through dollar signs. So Disney decided to quit selling out to the business world. He gave orders that all the corporation projects be cancelled and the companies be given their money back. He had an idea about Alaska and thought they ought to send a film crew up. Not only that, he thought he'd go along.

Disney was back on the right track. He wasn't sure exactly what he was doing or where it would lead, but it felt right and he trusted his instincts.

The Alaskan adventure produced *Seal Island,* the first in a series of half hour "True-Life Adventures." Of course, everyone told Disney no one would be interested in a half-hour nature movie. And, of course, everyone was wrong. *Seal Island* went on to win an Oscar for Short Documentary in 1948. However, it didn't do much to ease the studio's financial problems. Nevertheless, Disney was buoyed up, and he continued work on three feature-length films—*Peter Pan, Cinderella,* and *Alice in Wonderland.* He also started production on a non-animated feature film, *Treasure Island,* and began outlining his idea for an amusement park that he was thinking of calling Mickey Mouse

Park. His brother was dead set against the idea, for obvious financial reasons.

By 1950, the tide had turned. *Cinderella* was a great success (the first real film for the baby-boom generation) and *Treasure Island* was also making money. The second "True-Life Adventure," *Beaver Valley*, was enthusiastically accepted, and Disney's thoughts began turning toward the new medium of television. He agreed to do a Christmas special for NBC that year, and in 1951 he did another. At that time, he became fascinated with miniatures and experimented with making tiny mechanical scenes. But he realized there was no money to be made in his miniature replicas, since there was no way for many people to view them, so he turned his attention back to his concept of an amusement park. (As you've probably already recognized, those miniatures were the root idea for the oversized mechanical replicas that are an integral part of Disneyland.)

By now his brother, Roy, had gotten involved, and they made a lucrative deal with ABC. The plans for both the park and the television program were announced in April of 1954. Disney had surveys done to find the ideal location for Disneyland. He knew what he wanted, and just how he wanted it, and despite the cost, he was going to do it right—down to the last detail. And he did.

The moral of this story is:

Believe in yourself, believe in your dreams, and work your butt off to get there. Funding is always going to be a problem when you start out. Often, the more successful you become, the bigger your financial headaches are. But does it matter? You have to do what you want to do. There's no reason to stop, because no one can achieve your vision except you. Setbacks are only difficult at the time; you know they can't go on forever. When you look at the story of your life, they'll be interesting asides as they are in the Hershey and Disney histories. Get through them, put them behind you, and keep following your instincts.

Perseverance always pays off. But you have to go for it with your *heart* as well as your *head*.

When I was trying to launch my magazine, I was busy selling (or at least trying to sell) advertising space to every company connected with the entertainment industry. It was easy enough to pick up little ads from small neighborhood restaurants and discos, but I needed to catch some big fish.

I kept running into the same roadblock. All the big companies wanted to know my *demographics*. They wanted to know who my readers were and what market *Nightlife* was aimed at. I told them, but it wasn't enough. Finally, Dean Pearson, the head of R.J. Reynolds, took me aside and told me that no national company was going to make an advertising commitment without first "seeing my Simmons." I knew he wasn't talking about mattresses. What he meant was that I should hire Simmons, the largest independent research auditing agency—and known throughout the industry as the best—to do a demographic survey of my fledgling readership. Otherwise, I'd never get the advertising clients I needed.

What choice did I have? After all, it was only

money—money I didn't have, of course. I dug myself deeper into debt. My wife took a second job. And I got the Simmons. I sent it to Mr. Pearson and he called to say, "Son, if these figures are correct, and we're going to have them verified, you have a gold mine on your hands."

So I got the advertising support of R.J. Reynolds.

I learned that Experience has to come before Results. You pick up all sorts of information and useful knowledge every day. I'm sure all of you have read about a great sale at some time in your lives. The ads said the door opened at nine and closed at midnight. So you went over in the afternoon, thinking there would be several super bargains just waiting for you. And of course, they were all out of anything you had any interest in buying.

Now, one could say you failed to achieve your goal because you didn't come home with the bargains you set out for. But you learned something. You learned what it means when someone says, "the early bird catches the worm." You learned that if you want something, you have to get there first. And hopefully, you learned not to make the same mistake twice.

This kind of lesson can be applied to anything. You have to decide what you want to do, and then you have to do it! What's so hard about that?

Now it's time to take the initiative. All the self-help books in the world are only telling you what you already know. You can be talented, bright, attractive, self-confident, creative, and imaginative, and still be sitting on your duff . . .

Motivation doesn't come from the outside, no matter how many articles you read or how many motivational seminars you take. It all comes from *inside*. Your common sense takes over and says, "What are you waiting for?" And only you can answer that one . . .

## OUT OF THE MOUTHS OF BABES

Wisdom and common sense sometimes come out of the mouths of babes. One day I was sitting on the couch watching TV while my wife was trying to teach our son Mikey how to write. After an hour of frustration, my wife gently suggested they give it a rest, since Mikey's penmanship was terrible. Mikey, who was in the first grade at the time, shrugged and said, "Who cares? When I grow up, I'll hire a secretary just like Daddy, and she can write for me with a typewriter!"

My wife and I looked at each other and burst out laughing. I was proud of Mikey—not because of the remark he made, but because he already had the ability and know-how to get the job done. He used common sense. Just because you cannot do that special job or duty personally, doesn't mean you can't see to it that the job gets done. You just have to find someone who can do it. The results are the same!

The problem with today's society is that too many people are trying to figure out what's wrong—when they should be spending more time trying to figure out what works!

If Mikey can use common sense to get to the heart of a problem at age six, you certainly can use the ideas

I've shared with you to help you positively and effectively communicate and make good decisions for a continually successful (success-filled) life!

Just remember these three simple thoughts:

YOU MUST MAKE THE EFFORT.
YOU MUST THINK POSITIVE.
WHY NOT YOU?

You don't want to say when you're seventy years old:

I SHOULD HAVE . . .
I COULD HAVE . . .
I WOULD HAVE . . .
BUT I DIDN'T . . .
AND NOW I CAN'T . . .
AND PROBABLY WON'T.

Remember, God gave us common sense and timing. It's up to us to know how to use them.

# BIBLIOGRAPHY

*One of a Kind: Milton Snavely Hershey,* by Charles Schuyler Castner, Hershey, Pa.: The Derry Literary Guild, 1983.

Walt Disney: An American Original, by Bob Thomas, New York: Simon and Schuster, 1976.